THE TRANS-DIMENSIONAL DREAM WEAVERS

Doug Huffman

ISBN 979-8-9897112-1-5 (paperback)
ISBN 979-8-9897112-0-8 (eBook)

Printed in the United States of America

Introduction

One of the oldest, most fascinating, and certainly one of the least understood subjects of all time, is that of *dreams* and the **dream** *state*. Myriads of books have been written addressing the subject; even by such well known psychoanalysts as Sigmund Freud.

Being an avid dreamer myself, I have always found *dreaming* and *dreams* very *intriguing*, which prompted my reading of numerous books and listening to many lectures on the subject. My inevitable conclusion was; no one *really* understands dreams and what the dream state is really all about! There are many *plausible* notions and conclusions that have been and are currently tossed about, but in my opinion, *none* (of the so- called experts) has a *real* clue!

The reason I can be so dogmatic concerning the overall *cluelessness* of the experts is **personal** *experience*; not only of **prophetic** *dreams*, but such bizarre occurrences as "*remote viewing*" (*dreams*) or what I had come to label "*night visions*". After all, imagine the shock of discovering you have literally been in someone else's head, seeing through their eyes, in those **so-called** *dreams*!

I had previously assumed these *strange* night visions were typical *nonsensical* dreams until I by chance encountered a person involved in one of them and mustered the courage to ask her about it!. What a shocking and insightful discovery that literally changed everything I believed about dreams and dreaming! In the ensuing years, I was able to verify a few other "*remote viewing*" dream experiences as well; that is, observing things through the eyes of complete *strangers* I had *never* seen or *met*!

Interestingly, a movie was produced in 2012 around this whole *remote viewing phenomenon* called, "*Men who stare at goats*".

The basis of the movie was the militaries' *attempt* (in the 60's) to *train* people with this bizarre *ability* (l ike myself) to *harness* and *control* it. Unfortunately, the program was mostly *unsuccessful* and **supposedly** *canceled* due to little or *no **real** progress.*

But for me, discovering the reality and mechanics behind these bizarre occurrences certainly cracked the lid of a whole new level of insight into understanding *dreaming* and the **dream** *state.* We will venture into that very strange aspect of dreaming as well as the equally strange "*prophetic*" in upcoming chapters. But, before going there, it is noteworthy to point out the fact that ancient cultures and peoples, unlike us today, put great stock in *dreams* and dreaming. What did they know that we have lost?

These ancient cultures included Babylonian, Egyptian, Persian, Greek, Roman, and of course, one much closer to us; Native American Indian! In fact, one of the Native Americans' most recognized icons is the "*Dream Catcher*".

The Native Americans believed (and still believe to a degree) the dream catcher would catch the **bad** *dreams,* while allowing the **good** *dreams* to **pass** *through*! Interestingly, such faith in the dream catcher shows (**proves**) they believed dreams do **not** *originate from us,* but **outside** *us*! Again, is that ancient knowledge that has been lost in the dusty *shelves* of time?

I am reticent to debate the *validity* of the Native American's beliefs, but one *aspect* which I have personally *discovered* and *proven* quite *correct* is that many (if not all) dreams, do indeed "**not** *originate*" with us!

A dream *not* originating from our own minds is quite a shocking declaration, but is the ***only*** honest *explanation* for the ***prophetic*** and/or ***out of body*** *dreams*! After all, how do we explain someone ***seeing*** events in a *dream* that ***haven't*** *happened* and *people* they have ***never*** *met,* and then meet, unless these dreams don't *originate* with us?

That is a very *weighty* question to which there are myriads of *theories* and *opinions*, unfortunately few (if any) have held up to *serious* scrutiny such as my own personal experiences.

Again, considering the shocking and unbelievable dream and vision experiences I have personally experienced, what *options* do I have? I could just *pretend* they *didn't'* ***happen*** and/or that they are *normal*; or I could write a book and share these experiences with whomever is interested; maybe helping them better understand their *experiences* as well?

That said; I will be sharing many dreams and night visions including personal *remote viewing* and *prophetic* in upcoming chapters, but first, it will be very helpful to investigate some *ancient* examples of ***prophetic*** *dreaming*. After all, we can be very assured my experiences in strange dream phenomena are nothing new!

Contents

Chapter 1

Ancient Evidence

Some of the *oldest,* if not *the* oldest, examples of dreams, especially the *prophetic,* are found in a very *unexpected* but rather *obvious* place, the Bible. Whether or not one puts stock in the Bible (and/or Bible dreams) we can be sure of one thing; those *accounts* **originated** *somewhere*!

In fact, it was my personally *seeing* and *experiencing* so many *prophetic* dreams *paralleling* Bible accounts (in real time) that left me **no** *choice* but to place a very *high* level of **validity** in the Bible accounts. Also *reinforcing* my stand on those Bible accounts are the dozens of **miraculous** prayers **answered** and *miracles* I have personally *witnessed* and *experienced*! In fact, the *miraculous* has literally been and still is "*the norm*" for me.

My experience of dozens of **extra-dimensional** events, not only *erased* absolutely every shred of doubt of the parallel (higher) dimension that *exists* all around us, but led to writing a book series entitled; *The Trans-Dimensional Puppet Masters*! The *footprints* and *fingerprints* of other- dimensional beings can *be,* and **are** *found,* literally *everywhere* we look; we need only *open* our *eyes* and **see** *what* is *right* in *front* of our *faces.* After all "**willing** *ignorance*"; those who **refuse** to *see,* are the **truly** *ignorant*!

Considering ancient dreams *in* or *related* to the Bible, is one recorded by Enoch, the seventh born from Adam. (Genesis) The **Book of Enoch** incidentally, was part of the Bible canon until the church *hierarchy* **chose** to **remove** *it* (for lack of space) from the *authorized* collection in the second century CE. Unfortunately, after being *removed*, it acquired the status of *unauthorized* and was later ***demonized*** as *illegitimate*.

Sadly, the removal of *Enoch* from the Bible (OT) canon was one of the greatest travesties ever to *befall* mankind. The knowledge from Enoch that was *lost* (removed) was *truly* **breathtaking**! But, the ***good*** *news* is the **Book of Enoch** was *found* and is once again available for anyone so inclined to *restore* the *stock* and *faith* once *placed* in it!

The Book of **Enoch** alone, if *reauthorized*, and *taught,* would literally ***change*** the *face* of the world, especially its *religions*! Contained within its pages are vast amounts of *knowledge* detailing *world* ***changing*** *events* that transpired in *ancient* times (think shocking and still *unexplained, wonders* of the ***ancient*** world) and how our world came to ***think***, *behave* and ***be*** the *way* it is!

Also, add what the Bible has recorded (actually says without private interpretations) and you have the most shocking and mind-blowing *history, present,* and *future* one could possibly imagine! (Or not imagine) After all, it is said; "*The truth is stranger than fiction*"; an axiom I can personally vouch for, and if anything; an understatement! That said; Enoch lends majorly to understanding of *dreams* and their *origins*.

In chapter 84 of the Book of **Enoch**, Enoch relates a dream (vision) which not only laid out the *past* (before his time) but also a few *thousand* years into the *future*. Aside from that amazing *prophetic* aspect (proven true) it is also extremely fascinating to note the use of *symbolism*; especially in understanding the *construction* and *meaning* (purpose) of dreams! (*Think; "game of charades"*)

The symbolism in Enoch can greatly help in understanding our own dreams *here* and *now*. In fact, the *symbolic* nature (use of) of *dreaming* is a facet of dreaming virtually every dream expert *agrees* upon!

The following then, are few relevant versus from the "*Ethiopic Book of Enoch*" (beginning with chapter 84) *establishing* that extensive *use* of **symbolism**, as well as the *prophetic* aspect in dreams.

*"Enoch arose and said to his son Methuselah: to thee my son, will I speak. Hear my word and incline thine ear to the **visionary dream** of thy father. Before I married thy mother Edna, I saw a* (nite) *vision on my bed and beheld a cow sprung forth from the earth and this cow was white.*

Afterwards, a female heifer sprung forth and with it another heifer; one of them was black and one was red. The black heifer then struck the red one and pursued it on the earth.

From that period, I could see nothing more of the red heifer, but the black one increased in bulk and a female heifer came (went) *with him.*

After this, I saw that many cows proceeded forth resembling him and following after him. The first female young one also went out in the presence of the first cow and sought the red heifer, but found him not; and she lamented with a great lamentation while she was seeking him. Then I looked until that first cow came to her from which time she became silent and ceased to lament. Afterwards, she calved another white cow, and again, calved many cows and black heifers."

At this point, I would like to pause and *point* out some of the *symbolism* we have encountered in this dream; much of which is obvious to anyone knowing **Genesis**. This is the story of Adam (the first cow) and Eve (the first heifer) and her two sons, *Cain* and *Able* (black and red heifers).

The *black* (unrighteous) *heifer* is Cain who *murders* the *red* (righteous) *heifer*, Able. Then Eve (female heifer) searches for Able but doesn't find him (Cain got rid of the body). Then the *"first"* white *cow* (Adam) came and consoled her, where she then goes on to have many more children.

Another point that stands out was how the *black* heifer (Cain) apparently *married* and increased in bulk (power--Genesis points out that he built cities) and had many offspring.

Interestingly, we can only guess as to why *animals* were *used* to **depict** *humans* in that night vision (dream) but, this is not always the case as we will see shortly in The Pharaoh of Egypt's prophetic dream. (Gen.41).

In the Pharaohs' dream, *cows* were used to *depict*, **non human** *entities*, like *harvests*; both *lean* (bad) and *prosperous*, not people. Interestingly, if we use the Bible as our *interpretation* key, an *animal* most often used to *depict* **people**, is *sheep*, in contrast to Enoch's using *cows*. Maybe it was because people in ancient times were *stronger* (lived to be almost a thousand years old)?

My personal opinion is that it is *not* the *animals* or the *people* that are the object lesson of such dreams as Enoch's, but *show* **where** *things* **began** and **where** *they* were *going*. In fact, many children's *movies* and *shows* use animals (even cars or vegetables) to *teach* children *lessons* about life, which makes one wonder; did that *idea* come from the *same* **place** as *our* **dreams**?

Actually, chapter 85 of Enoch conveys that very point! Let's look!

"Again I looked with my eyes while sleeping, and surveyed heaven above; and behold a single star (not human) *fell from heaven, which being raised up, ate and fed among the cows.*

*After that, I perceived other large and black cows and beheld all of them **changed** their stalls and pastures, while their young began to lament one with another.*

Again I looked in my vision and surveyed heaven; when behold I saw many stars which descended and projected themselves from heaven to where the first star was."

I'd like to pause here and comment about the *new* symbol (entity) *injected* here; it's a **star** that *falls* from *heaven* and takes up residence with the black cows (descendants of Cain).

Obviously, the black cows are associated with Cain and his descendants, but "*what*" are the *stars*? Well, we need only continue a little further and *combine* that with other Bible keys to understand! **Enoch** 85:5

*"Into the midst of those young ones, while the cows were with them feeding in the midst of them, I looked at and observed them, when behold, they all protruded their parts of shame like horses and began to ascend the young cows; all of whom became pregnant and brought forth **elephants, camels**, and **asses**!"*

Before getting to the stars, we notice *a **new** symbol* is introduced; the *offspring* the **stars** *produced* with the cows! The Bible (and Enoch) is faithful in *providing* the needed *keys* to *unlocking* the dream *symbols* in **Genesis** 6 and **Enoch** 7 respectively.

Genesis calls these "*stars*" the "*sons of God*", while Enoch (the parallel version) calls them "*Watchers*" and "*Angels*". Their **highbred** *offspring* then (between Angels and humans) are called "*Nephilim*"; translated "*giants*".

Of course, a little further research reveals *"giants"* to be a *poor* translation at best considering **Psalms** 147:4 tells us that the Creator calls all the *stars* by **name** and that they *all* **sang** *together* at the *creation* of the Earth (and mankind) in **Job** 38:7. We also see there the *stars* called the *"Sons of God"* as well.

So, at this point, we have the *"stars"* called *"sons of God"*, as well as *"angels"*. But, as an interesting, although *relevant* aside, one more shocking description is given us in **Genesis** 1:20-25. There we find the animals all being *created "according to* (in the likeness) *its kind"*! Well, after a very basic Bible study, we find the **only** kinds **pre**-existing mankind was the *Creator* (YHWH) and His *Angels*!

So, if the *animals* were created **after** *their* **kind**, it could only have been the **Angelic** *kind*! Yes, animals *exist* in Heaven (adjacent dimension) according to **Genesis** 1! But, that's another subject. (See "The Transdimensional Puppet Masters" v. 2) Don't forget; the creature that **spoke** *to* and *deceived* Eve, was an *animal* (*"beast of the field"* Gen. 2)

Continuing on, we see the nephilim offspring between those *stars* (angels; animal-watchers) and *cows* spawned a **new** *symbol* or *entity* in the dream; *"**unclean** animals"*! Until the **stars** *descended*, there were only *"clean"* animals (*cows*) until the *mixing* of the *angel* and *human* DNA created the unclean *elephants, camels,* and asses!

What an interesting coincidence that the mascots for our political party's (in the US) are none other than **elephants** and **asses**!

Plus; is it also only a weird fluke of *chance* that the ancients, virtually across the board, *worshipped* **animals** (and half animal-humans) as *gods*? Not a *chance*!

At any rate, we find the list of *unclean* (non eatable) and clean (eatable) listed in the Bible book of **Leviticus** chapter 11. Incorporating those angelic (star) symbols of Enoch's dream, it is obvious that *"clean and unclean"* have a much deeper meaning than simple animal *flesh*!

In that regard I would like to quote one last segment of Enoch's dream that *introduces* yet one more symbol to consider! **Enoch** 86;

"Again I perceived them when they began to strike and to swallow (eat) *each other and the earth cried out. Then I raised my eyes a second time towards heaven and saw a vision, that behold, there came forth from heaven as it were the likeness of* **white men**. *One came forth from thence and three with him.*

v.3 Then they shewed me a lofty tower on the earth while every hill became diminished. And they said: Remain here until thou perceive what shall come upon those **elephants**, *camels, and* **asses**, *upon the* **stars**, *and upon all the cows.*

Then I looked at that one of the four white men who came forth first. He seized the first **star** *which* **fell** (descended) *down from heaven and binding* **it** *hand and foot, he cast* **it** *into a valley: a valley narrow, deep, stupendous and gloomy.*

Then one of them drew his sword and gave it to the elephants, camels, and asses, who began to strike each other, and the whole earth shook on account of them.

And when I looked in the vision; behold one of those four angels, who came forth, hurled from heaven, collected together and took all the great **stars** *whose parts of shame resembled those of horses; and binding them all hand and foot, cast them into the cavities of the earth!"*

Again, the main point for showing these portions of Enoch's dream is to show the *mix* of symbols, both *literal* and *metaphoric*, and most of all; the *prophetic*. Enoch goes on to further relate in his dream, the great flood. Let's continue in chapter 88;

"Then one of those four (white men-angels) *went to the white cows and taught them a mystery. While the cow was trembling, it was born and became a man and fabricated for himself a large ship* (Noah's Ark)*"*.

v. 4; "*The water began to boil up and rose over the earth so that the village was not seen while its whole soil was covered with water. Much water was over it, darkness, and clouds. Then I surveyed the height of this water and it was elevated above the village. It flowed over the village and stood higher than the earth.*

Then all the cows which were collected there while I looked upon them were drowned; swallowed up and destroyed in the water. But the ship floated above it. All the cows, the elephants, the camels, and the asses (nephilim) *were drowned on the earth.*"

Enoch was *prophesying* the great flood, which happened hundreds of years after he related this dream to his son *Methuselah*. In fact, according to an ancient Hebrew expert I heard lecture, the name "*Methuselah*" literally means; "*When he dies, it* (the flood) *will come*"!

And, that's exactly what the Bible recorded happened! The great flood came immediately *after* Methuselah's death at almost a *thousand* years. Enoch was long gone (from Earth) hundreds of years before that!

Enoch's dream goes on to outline the next few thousand years of humanities' history where interestingly, people eventually began to be *depicted* as *sheep* and *goats* instead of cows. Apparently, people were *no longer* what they *used* to *be*!? (Pun intended!)

Chapter 2

Prophetic Biblical Dreams

We will change gears a little and take a look at some more *prophetic* dreams shown in the Bible, which are also very telling. Beginning in **Genesis** 37, where we find Joseph, the youngest son of Jacob (Israel) at about 17 years of age.

In verse 6, Joseph (his father's favorite son) was telling his brothers a *dream* he had. Obviously, that was *not* the *smartest* thing he could have done, considering it got him *sold* into *slavery*. Let's read it beginning in verse 6;

"Now Joseph dreamed a dream and he told it to his brothers and they hated him even more." (Jealousy)

V.7 (Joseph tells his dream) "*There we were binding sheaves in the field. Then behold, my sheaf arose and also stood upright and indeed your sheaves stood all around and bowed down to my sheaf.*"

V.9 *Then he dreamed still another dream and told it to his brothers and said; "Look, I have dreamed another dream. And this time, the sun, the moon, and the eleven stars bowed down to me."*

Interestingly, we see previous symbols *changed* to *something* **different**. This shows something very crucial; symbols are *defined* by *context*; literal or not.

Chapter 3

Progressive v. Recurring Dreams

Reading on, we discover Joseph's dreams landed him in *slavery* and ultimately *prison* where he was once again was *confronted* with *dream* issues. While there, it seems the Pharaoh's *butler* and *baker* were both *accused* of trying to *kill* the king and were thrown in the prison with Joseph. While there, they both related dreams they had to Joseph. **Genesis** 40:5

"Then the butler and the baker of the king of Egypt, who were confined in the prison dreamed a dream; both of them, each man's dream in one night and each man's dream with its own interpretation.

And Joseph came in to them in the morning and looked at them and saw they were sad. So he asked Pharaoh's officers who were with him in the custody of his lord's house saying; "Why do you look so sad today"? And they said to him; we each have dreamed a dream and there is no interpreter of it."
And Joseph said to them; "Do not interpretations belong to YHWH? (KJ-*the Lord*)

Tell them to me, please. Then the chief butler told his dream to Joseph and said to him; "Behold, in my dream a vine was before me and in the vine were three branches; it was as though it budded, its blossoms shot forth ripe grapes. Then the Pharaoh's cup was in my hand and I took the grapes and pressed them into Pharaoh's cup and placed the cup in Pharaoh's hand.

And Joseph said to him; "this is the interpretation of it; the three branches are three days. Now within three days, Pharaoh will lift up your head and restore you to your place and you will put Pharaoh's cup in his hand according to the former manner when you were his butler."

"When the chief baker saw that the interpretation was good, he said to Joseph; "I also was in my dream and there I had three white baskets on my head. In the uppermost basket there were all kinds of baked goods for Pharaoh and the birds ate them out of the basket on my head.

So Joseph answered and said; "This is the interpretation of it; the three baskets are three days.

"Within three days Pharaoh will lift off your head from you and hang you on a tree and the birds will eat your flesh from you."

To make a long story a little *shorter*, the dreams were indeed *prophetic* and *happened* exactly as Joseph *predicted*, but unfortunately, the butler's *promise* to mention Joseph's **unjust** incarceration to the Pharaoh, was *forgotten* until a couple years later when the Pharaoh also had a dream.

Suddenly the butler remembered his *promise* to Joseph and told the Pharaoh who then had Joseph brought in. (Gen.41:16)

"And the Pharaoh said to Joseph; "I have dreamed a dream and there is no one who can interpret it. But I have heard it said of you that you can understand a dream, to interpret it.

V.17 "Then Pharaoh said to Joseph; "Behold, in my dream I stood on the bank of the river. Suddenly seven cows came up out of the river, fine looking and fat and they fed in the meadow.

Then behold, seven other cows came up after them, poor and very ugly and gaunt, such ugliness as I have never seen in all the land of Egypt. And the gaunt and ugly cows ate up the first seven, the fat cows.

When they had eaten them up, no one would have known that they had eaten them, for they were just as ugly as at the beginning, so I awoke.

Also I saw in my dream and suddenly seven heads came up on one stalk (of wheat) *full and good. Then behold, seven heads, withered thin and blighted by the east wind, sprang up after them. And the thin heads devoured the seven good heads."*

Then Joseph said to Pharaoh; "The dreams of Pharaoh are one; YHWH has shown Pharaoh what He is about to do. The seven good cows are seven years and the seven good heads are seven years; the dreams are one.

V.29 "Indeed seven years of great plenty will come throughout all the land of Egypt but after them seven years of famine will deplete the land. So the plenty will not be known in the land because of the famine following, for it will be very severe."

As it turns out, the Pharaoh believed Joseph and put him in *charge* of *storing* food during the *good* years in order to survive the 7 *bad* years. And, sure enough, everything played out exactly as the *dreams* **predicted** which brings everything back to Joseph's *original* dreams!

Before the famine ended, Joseph's family ended up coming to Egypt to buy grain and would you believe, *bowed* down to Joseph. He was now after all, the second in power in Egypt under the Pharaoh! Bottom line; those prophetic dreams did **not** *originate* from the *brains* of those that had them; they were *obviously* **given** *from* an **outside** source!

You may not believe the Bible stories, but I personally am unable to *ignore* them considering the many *prophetic* dreams of my own I've experienced; that is, coming to pass exactly as I was given them!

In the next chapters, I will share some of them including another *strange* and **rarely** *experienced* dream *state* (type) *"progressive"*!

One of the more *odd* and *rare* dream sequences I have experienced is **progressive** *dreaming*. Progressive dreaming is where a dream picks up where an earlier dream left off. This type of dreaming is not to be confused with *recurring* dreams. Recurring dreams are the **same** *dream* or *some* **element** of a dream *repeated* over and over.

Recurring dreams are quite *common* and will be addressed more fully a little later, but this chapter is *dedicated* to dream *patterns* that *build* upon *past* dreams and continue to *move* **forward** in *linier fashion,* just as in real life. Recurring dreams are about us being *stuck* somewhere until something *changes*.

The truth is, the only dreams I paid much attention to early on were my *recurring* dreams; like *flying*; showing up in school *naked,* or not being able to find my English classroom. I personally believe **recurring** *dreams* are about *grabbing* our *attention* but mine wasn't peaked until after forty when my **progressive** and *prophetic* dreams prompted me to begin *recording* them.

Upon doing so, the most amazing thing was to see my *dream* **life** literally *explode*. It was as if my *paying* **attention** to my dreams got the *attention* of the "**dream weavers**". I can't explain who the *dream weavers* are exactly, but what I can say (from experience) was that their *attention* was certainly *gained* once I began *logging* my dreams!

I use the term "*dream weavers*" a bit loosely, but I can vouch for that reality; not only my prophetic dreams, but my answered *dream* **prayers** as well

The *answered* dream prayers began occurring a few years after I began recording my dreams. Once I realized that my dreams (at least most of them) were *not* originating with me, I began *praying* for certain dreams; *dream* **prayers** that would *regularly* be **answered**!

At this point, it's easy to conclude that my *prayer* dreams were *answered* simply because it was *what* I *wanted*; and that my mind was just *conjuring* them up. But, at least *two* of those dream prayers, once answered **regularly**, at one point *ceased* to be *answered*, no matter how much I *asked, begged, cajoled,* and/or *wished* them to happen. So much for my mind creating the dreams!

The dreams I was **praying** *for* no longer coming was one of the big *proofs* that our dreams are not **conjured** *up* by our own *will* and *minds*! This further **proves** the Native American Indians were *correct* in believing our dreams do indeed *come* from **outside** *us*!

That said; let me be perfectly clear; there can be no doubt our dreams are certainly <u>still connected to our</u> personal ***experiences*** and ***emotions***.

That is probably the main reason the **origin** of *dreams* is so *confusing*! It is my conclusion that the *dream weavers* use our *experiences* and *emotions* in their game of *dream* **charades** they *play* with us! (More on that later)

At this point, I would like to relate my *progressive* dream series, which began with a dream that took place in one of the cowyards on my childhood farm in South Dakota. But to set the stage I must first relate a *recurring* dream (the first I can remember) beginning at about 7 or 8.

In this recurring dream, I was always standing in my front yard of our old farmhouse, with the thought that if I tried hard enough, I could fly! I would then *flap* my arms (real hard) and sure enough, I would start *lifting* off the ground! I would always get about the *height* of the telephone wires, when I would begin to tire and come down.

But, looking down, there was always a *big,* **black**, and **vicious**, *animal* waiting for me, so I would put everything I had into staying up! Inevitably, I would keep dropping until in *horror,* would abandon my efforts to *exhaustion*! I would then awaken in a *sweat*!

That recurring front-yard flying dream never changed until my twenties, when I suddenly got the notion to fly again; instead of standing in our front yard, I found myself in the *southwest* **cowyard**. As I flapped my arms and rose from the ground, what a heart bursting joy to see that I wasn't *tiring* as I *rose* like a bird; so high, I was up where the jets fly!

Just before waking, I found myself soaring in the warm soft sunshine over the beautiful blue Baja peninsula of Mexico! Interestingly, it seems the dream come to fruition when I left the farm and moved to the Southwest, where I was never to experience that *recurring* flying dream again.

Interesting, virtually all dream experts agree that *flying* is symbolic of *freedom*, which I also concur. You see, the farm had always felt like a *work* **prison** where I was given very **little** *time* to *play* which felt like a work camp! Again, it wasn't until I moved to the southwest that the *recurring* dreams of not being able to *fly* **away** from the farm *ended*!

In the following 20 years I don't remember having any *farmhouse* dreams until the *progressive* farmhouse dreams began; and with an undeniable religious element jumping out right in the beginning!

Who knows; maybe it had something to do with the fact that I had been very *interested* and **involved** *with* church until I was excommunicated (over doctrinal issues) around the *millennial* turn.

Ironically, I was afterwards, miraculously reacquainted with some people from my past in a home Bible study. One of them had a cousin who was a minister, which we began listening to via telephone link up for a while.

I had never seen (except possibly a picture) met, or talked to the man until I had the **first** of my *progressive* **farmhouse** *dreams*. That is where things got extremely interesting as I'm about to show you!

The dream opened with a beautiful, warm, sunny, day where people were milling about in small groups talking in the southeast cowyard of my childhood farm. The atmosphere was very peaceful until an old *horse* drawn *medicine **show** wagon* careened through the south fence screeching to a *halt* in middle of the cowyard.

I thought it was strange that no one seemed to notice, so I went over to get a closer look. On the west side of the wagon, I was looking at what looked like a row of four (chicken) laying boxes, when suddenly, a movement caught my eye. Taking a closer look, I detected a rat or weasel hiding! So I found a stick and proceeded to *kill* it!

The commotion, culminating in my holding up the dead vermin, caused people to begin gathering around in curiosity, but then they began moving around to the back of the wagon, so I tossed the rodent aside and went to see what was so interesting.

In the middle of the dirty *dilapidated **medicine*** wagon, was a man dressed in a dark expensive looking suit! Since the back of the wagon was too small to stand up in, he was just squatting there. He appeared to want to come out, but I could see he was apprehensive. So I climbed in and sat down in front of him and began talking. I have to say that I was very impressed at how humble he ***seemed*** to be but I was still unable to talk him out of the wagon!

Even though I had never seen or met this man in person, I instantly knew who he was; the minister we had been listening to! So I decided to attend one of his services a couple weeks later and sure enough, it was him right down to his dark suit!

Well, what shocked me most was when after telling some other friends of going to one of his services, a woman exclaimed; *"Stay away from him, he's a con man"*! As it turns out this woman's friend, who was also a mutual friend of mine, had been cheated out of 60 grand by that man!

I couldn't believe my ears considering the dream I had of him showing up in the southeast cowyard of the farmhouse in a dilapidated old *medicine* wagon! Virtually everyone (in the day) considered the owners of medicine wagons to be **charlatans**! Amazingly, *time* **proved** the woman (and my dream) to be correct!

The medicine wagon incident was quite astounding, but it let me to an even more astonishing and related discovery; that my childhood farmhouse and yard were laid out in the same pattern as the Israelite temple in the Bible!

The farmhouses (like the Temples) were in the center with *fenced* (cow) yards (temple courtyards) all around. The main entrance, just as in the Bible, was from the east, with minor entrances from the south and north. Even the *destruction* of the **two** *farmhouses* matched the Bible pattern!

You see, Solomon's temple (the first temple) was *torn down* by the Babylonians just as the *first* (old) *farmhouse* was *torn down*. The *second* temple (Herod's) was *burned* by the Romans in 70 CE just as the *second* farmhouse was *burned*, forcing my parents off the farm! Then everything was completely leveled just as Jerusalem was leveled after the Roman general Titus conquered the city and *burned* it!

You may say it was all just an interesting coincidence, but my personal experiences say otherwise (to me)! At any rate, those supposed coincidences went a long way in helping me understand; not only *what* the progressive dreams were about, but that there is a **prophetic** *element* woven all through them as well!

I have no idea how many of the farmhouse dreams are prophetic until I can look back someday and say; "*Yes, that's what I saw*"! But, considering what happened in **real** *life* with the *medicine wagon* dream, I can say **that** with a large degree of confidence.

After that dream of the charlatan minister coming in from the southeast (US) to Zion (meaning "*Where YHWH the Creator dwells*") Utah, all playing out for *real,* set the stage for the coming progressive farmhouse dreams!

Again, the farmhouse in the dreams was a typical of *Zion* (the temple in Jerusalem) and that the minister who arrived in the medicine wagon finally settled (founded his little community) to the southeast of Zion, just as he came into the southeast cowyard of the farmhouse (in the dream)!

I will get back to more of those incredible progressive farmhouse dreams later, as the farmyard slowly grew into a huge city, but first would like to share some other personal prophetic dreams that played out exactly as I saw them; well before they happened.

Chapter 4

Personal Prophetic Dreams

In the first chapter we looked at some prophetic dreams found in the Bible (and Enoch) and how they came to fruition. But, such distant examples are very difficult to *identify* and *connect* with, but there were some personal ones in my life that are nothing short of *mind-blowing*!

I will share some of these beginning with one that happened on a Friday night after having checked into a motel in Springdale (Zion) Utah for a long weekend. I would go there to spend the annual Sabbath Feasts and to work on my writing.

The dream (night vision) opened with the scene of my brother (who works for in me in my construction business) and me digging a hole in the middle of a house I didn't recognize. But even though the house was strange, I knew it belonged to a couple we had done considerable work for in the past; but who I hadn't seen or talked to in a couple years.

The scene was crystal clear; we had broken up the concrete floor and were digging deep under it. We had dirt piled 2-3 feet deep all around the hole, which was the scene that ended the dream (night vision).

I gave the strange night vision little thought until a call came Sunday morning (while still in Zion two days later) from the wife of this very same couple! She was very excited about a house they had just bought and was wondering if I could come by and give them my evaluation before their three day right of rescission expired!

Needless to say, I thought it was an extremely interesting coincidence, especially considering they bought the house on Friday, the very night I had the vision! But what a surprise I was in for when I met them Monday to evaluate the house!

When I walked into this house, even though I had never been in it before, I instantly recognized it; it was the one in my Zion vision! But, I still didn't know what the breaking up the floor I had seen was all about; at least until I began checking out the plumbing in the house!

While investigating the water heater room, I could hear water running and after checking the house from end to end, found nothing. That's when it was confirmed; there was a broken pipe under the concrete floor! I didn't know where it was and told the couple they should talk to the sellers about it.

A few days later the woman called me again, and to make a long story short, we ended up breaking up the floor to work on the under-slab plumbing exactly where I saw in the night vision! That was an amazing prophetic dream, but certainly not the only one. The first one I remember having was many years before in 1998.

In that dream (night vision) I found myself standing in a compound of some sort, with high (so high I could barely see the top) white, stucco walls that seemed to go on forever into the horizon. Directly in front of me was a massive black steel (looking) door some sixteen feet wide, ten feet high, and looking to be about a foot thick.

As I stood there wondering where this strange place was, I heard voices all around lamenting in heartbreaking and hopeless tones; "*How will we ever get out, who can open the door?*" The terrible *despair* and *anguish* in their voices was so *powerful* I could literally feel it to the bottom of my soul.

As I was listening and wondering, I suddenly heard another voice behind me say, "*Heather has the key*", to which I responded; "*What do you mean Heather has the key*"?

Just then, I looked to see that the massive black steel door now had what looked like Bible verses written on it. The top half was English and the bottom appeared to be Spanish or something similar. As I was trying to read what the verses said, suddenly the door began to open! At the same time, a tumult of joyous cheering erupted all around!

Apparently, this compound with the beautiful white stucco walls was a prison and the prisoners had just been set free! Even so, I still had no idea what this *prison* the people in were *in **was***, and most especially; *why* I was there!?

As it just so happened, I knew a young woman in the church I attended with the same name; she was the piano player and I was the music leader (among other things). Naturally, I assumed she was the name I heard in the vision and could help shed light (had the key) on understanding what that night vision was all about.

I foolishly attempted to talk to her about it but as you might guess, she didn't want to hear any of it and certainly not talk about it, as I discovered!

The vision was so powerful; I just couldn't get it off my mind and was feeling desperate to understand what it meant. And, as the voice in the vision told me; "*Heather had the key*". So naturally, I kept trying to engage her about it. She never actually told me she didn't want to talk to me, but instead told our minister to tell me for her.

Our minister told me what she had said to him and ordered me to never talk or even attempt to talk to her again. It was then I realized I had *offended* her and felt obligated to at least send her an e-mail apology and to assure her that I would not bother her anymore.

But, by doing so, our minister felt I had crossed the line and told me I was no longer welcome in his congregation; a decree that was incredibly devastating considering church had always been my favorite place ever since I was little.

In fact, I had always been a glutton for more *Biblical* and *spiritual* understanding but it seemed the church had *hit* the *wall* of increasing knowledge. A few years earlier it had become apparent that there was no more for them to give; just constant *regurgitation* of the *same* **old** *understanding*.

Interestingly; after that, when I began *reading* and *studying* the Bible for what it **actually** *said* and not the *private* **interpretation** the church (churches) *coerced* us into *accepting* as truth, I was shocked! As it turns out, the Bible, when read for what it actually *says* (translation problems not withstanding) is the most shocking and *bizarre* book on the planet!!

In fact, what I found prompted to write a book about it called; "**Christianity; Great Hope or Hoax**"! I did an update almost ten years later called "**Christianity; Our Great Hope or Angelic Deception**", but bottom line; the *truth* in the Bible really is *"**stranger than fiction**"* when *accepted* for what it *actually* says!

It was in the writing of that book that I realized the *night* **vision** prison was actually a **prophecy** for me! You see, the **corporate** *religion* I was part of, *"was" the white* stucco **prison**! After all, unless a person *accepts* and *embraces* the particula r *"private interpretations"* of the Bible *church* or *denomination* (or minister) they *belong* to, they simply are **not** *welcome*!

That is in fact, the very reason there are hundreds of major Christian denominations; they all differ in their **private** *interpretations* of the Bible; literally **none** *accepting* it for what it *actually* teaches! Consequently, embracing the churches particular interpretations of the scriptures to *belong* (or go to hell) literally makes it a *prison*.

It seems the situation with Heather *set* me *free* from **corporate** *religion* which I **never** *ever* would have *left* on my *own*! It was *attempting* to **talk** to *her* about the vision that literally made her *"**the key**"* to *escaping* (being excommunicated) from that **corporate** *religious* **prison**.

But, according to the vision, it is not only me that is *set* **free** from that *prison* (I had no knowledge of being in) but apparently millions. In fact, it could even be billions who are eventually *set* **free** by the actual *truth* of the Bible!

In a related thought; it seems our dimension; i.e. our *environment* and existence is nothing more than a dimension *existing* **within** *another*; possibly even many other dimensions.

The theory is that each dimension vibrates at a different speed which renders a faster vibrating dimension *invisible* and *untouchable* to a *slower* one. The slower one is perceived in *slow motion* to the *faster* one, which makes those in the *faster* vibrating dimensions seem *supernatural* (to ours) and are easily viewed as *supernatural*!

That might seem like a bit of a deviation from the subject of *dreams* and *dreaming*, but I can assure you it is anything but; it is all very much **connected**! One thing is for sure, we are **not** *alone* in our *dimension* (reality)!

How difficult would it be for those in a faster vibrating dimension or existence to plant visions in our heads while we are sleeping? After all, it is said that in order for the other dimensions to communicate with us, our **conscience** *minds* have to be *out of the way*; like in *sleeping*!

With that in mind, there are just a couple more *prophetic* night visions I would like to share before moving on; the first of which took place in the Bumbleberry Motel in Springdale (Zion) Utah. I was there to attend the Feast of Tabernacles and was staying in room 222 and had gone to bed.

I was awakened around midnight by the sound of "*Maid*" outside my door. Knowing housekeeping didn't work that late, I figured I had just been dreaming and went back to sleep only to be awakened a *second* time by the *sound* of someone "*in*" my room!

I turned on the light to see a Hispanic woman in a maid's uniform going through my things. I demanded she tell me what she was doing and in her shock she began *apologizing* profusely, and *lamenting* about not having enough money to feed her children.

At the same time, she was pulling up the carpet and wrapping it around herself and swaying to some *inaudible, ethereal* music; as if she were Cinderella dreaming of the ball. It was all very strange and just then I woke up and realized that it was all just a dream (or night vision)!

The next morning, as I was driving out of the motel parking lot, what a shocking sight to see that same Hispanic housekeeper (whom I had never seen in *real* life) pushing a cart of towels across the parking lot toward the building I was staying in. To say I was shocked is the understatement of the century!

Overcome by curiosity, I parked my truck and followed her into the building to ask if she was the maid that cleaned my room 222. To my additional shock, she answered; "*yes*"! Feeling bad, I gave her 20 dollars and apologized for not leaving a tip every day (I was staying for a week).

After staying the rest of the week, I never saw her again and finally asked the Caucasian housekeeping crew what happened to her. To my utter amazement, they told me that there was no Hispanic maid working at that motel!

The bottom line; what I saw in my night vision, certainly did not come from me! Just exactly what was it I saw that next morning; an apparition or a *real* person? That certainly was a real 20 dollar bill I gave her though!

Considering this chapter, I must again *ask*; how do **our "own" minds** *conjure* up *images* and *details* we have *never* seen? After all, that is the most widely held belief about dreams! The prophetic dreams (night visions) I shared in this last chapter could not possibly have been dreamed up on my own (pun intended)!

Again, how is we can meet and have conversations with people in our dreams we have never seen or met in real life? But then; how do we *know* **what** we *see* in our dreams **isn't** *real* in *one way* or *another*; just in a way we are unable or *don't* **want** to understand?

With that thought in mind, and before moving on to the next chapter, I would like to share one last short little dream (night vision) about a friend of mine who lives in the next state.

Again, this was what I call a night vision; more like a *snapshot* (with sound effects) rather than a *rambling* or *nonsensical* dream. In it, I saw my friend sitting at her little desk by her kitchen with boxes piled high around her while at the same time looking very *frustrated* and *overwhelmed*.

So, the next morning, I called her and asked her how things looked and to my amazement, the scene she described was exactly what I saw in the night vision! She told me she was going through all these boxes of papers and things from the garage and was trying to sort and organize and was feeling very *exasperated*!

Chapter 5

Celebrity Dreams

At this point, and with the last chapter in mind, I would like to turn a slightly *whimsical* direction in the subject of dreams and night visions, which is those I have had with *celebrities*. These dreams (night visions) are very bizarre considering the celebrities I *met* in them I have never seen or encountered in **real** *life,* nor necessarily had any desire to! In fact, a few of them, I don't even like!

But, if nothing else, these celebrity night visions were very interesting considering they were as *real* as my *regular* day before was! It was as I was in someone else's bodies; like the *"remote viewing"* experiences I've had and been able to confirm! I will go into those in a later chapter.

This *first* celebrity dream (vision) I'm relating was the *first* I remembered and *wrote* down and probably **not** the *first* of such dream *episodes*. It happened in April of 2007 and had *nothing* to do with what I had *watched* on TV or thought about in the recent past preceding the night vision.

It opened with my arrival at what appeared to be a fairly new housing development considering there was no landscaping or trees, just big expensive looking homes. I arrived at one and was shown to my room by someone I didn't know (who seemed to know me) and went to bed.

The next morning, I came downstairs to find the very well known actor (I will call *Denny*) sitting at a little breakfast table between the kitchen and living room in his bathrobe. He looked up to see me and motioned me to come sit with him and have some tea.

Denny and I sat and had a nice conversation (which I forgot because I didn't write it down soon enough) but it was as if were old and dear friends. What I do remember though, is how amiable he was; very **different** *from* what I personally *believed* him to be! (From TV and the movies)

Again, what impacted me most about that dream is that I have never met Denny nor have ever seen him interviewed, yet the dream (night vision) was as real as what had happened just the day before. Again; did my mind really *fabricate* those **precise** *details* of him and his house especially since it was *not* what I previously *believed* about him?

Such dreams (night visions) have to prompt one to consider if there wasn't *something* **real** *involved*. In view of that specific dream, there is no way (for me) to know; although it would be rather interesting to meet him, see his house inside and out, just to *verify* any connection to *reality*!

In this next celebrity dream (night vision) my wife and I had gone to meet a real-estate agent (and his client) to look at a house (mansion) by the beach she was interested in buying. It was quite a surprise to see the woman with the realtor and seller (apparently his ex-wife) was none other than a well known actress I will call "*Jan*".

The seller and agent got into a debate, so Janie asked me if she could show me the house. In spite of the fact that it was a beautiful and expensive house, I was surprised at how low quality the furnishings were. It looked as if someone had just done a low-budget decorating job just for the sale.

At any rate, Jan was flirting with me and asked if I wanted to see the back yard and beach while we were waiting, to which I agreed. That ended the dream, but interestingly I looked in the paper the next morning and was shocked see a picture of her in the newspaper (flirting with someone) looking exactly like she did to me in the dream!

Again, how was that possible? It was after the dream I saw her picture in the paper looking like she did in the dream, not before! In fact, I'd swear the picture of her was taken while she was with me at that beach house! Obviously, it wasn't me there, but who? Is it possible I was simply looking through the eyes of the one who was buying the house in *real* life?

That is a heady question, which on a few occasions I have been able to verify. I have personally confirmed that such *phenomena* as *seeing* through *someone **else's'** eyes* in ***real** time* is possible and does happen in real time; again, it is a scientifically confirmed phenomena called "*Remote viewing*".

Those celebrity night visions were extremely interesting and worthy of sharing but I have more that add additional *intrigue* and *mystery* to this whole notion of ***where** dreaming* and *dreams **come** from*. This next one was especially intriguing considering the *politics* involved!

This night vision opened with my standing in front of a department store in a large city, which had the feel of New York. I was apparently on some kind of rant (political?) when I saw another famous actress I will call "*Goldie*" (not Goldie Hawn) walk past into a department store.

Inside, she *turned* a clothes rack that caused a *secret* door to *open*, which as it turned out, was the entrance to some sort of apartment in the back of the store. I followed her in where she turned and gave me a hug and kiss on the cheek. Then I sat down at a long table in a large room where another famous actor I will call "*Deni*" (not the same as the other one) was also seated.

I struck up a conversation and asked him what he did for fun. His face lit up and he said, "*I know just the game*", which he went to get. Then he gathered a group of children together and began to have them act out commands he was gave them. Strangely, the game was apparently called "*The Constitution*"!

Again, the implications of that dream are quite intriguing! Was any of it *based* in *reality*; or was it all simply **contrived** *nonsense*? On the other hand; was it metaphorical like the Biblical dream in the first chapter? But, one thing is for sure, it was as *real* for me (even more-so) than what had happened to me the day before!

The reason I speculate symbolism may be involved (although mixed with reality) is the connection with *politics*. After all, politics has been a very *common* theme in my dreams and visions.

This next short but shocking night vision really brings that concept home! It was about the man who was "*supposed **to be**"* Pope. This very strange dream opened with a friend (I've never seen or met in this life) and me following the iron-man triathlon.

The triathlon had come to the *swim* event and I was leaning on an ocean side patio rail watching a middle-aged man we were following and commented to the other man with me; "*Did you know he* (the one swimming) *was supposed to be the pope*"(instead of Francis)?

What a shock that was considering the dream occurred in December of 2013, not long after Pope Francis had been inaugurated! Again, the *political* overtones are *obvious* and it makes one wonder *where* it is *coming from* and how much *reality* is involved, *literally* or *metaphorically*? That dream seemed pretty blatant in its political nature, but some are much more whimsical such as the afternoon (in a night vision) with a very famous Australian actor.

My dream with him in 2006; again, was rife with incredible *detail* and opened in a small town amidst a town celebration of some sort. I had been watching a tent play and had left to use the port-a-potty when I saw this actor I will call "*Mac*" sitting on a nearby bench with a teenage boy. It felt like I had met him before, so I went over and said "*Hi*" and asked him about being Catholic and how he was being treated after one of his recent movies.

He started to tell me but got side-tracked with a rant about a couple movie extras (in a new movie) that caused him a great deal of trouble. Getting increasingly upset by the minute, he finally stormed off to his car.

The boy and I followed and got in the front seat with him. In his anger and frustration, Mac careened around the streets, squealing around every corner until I finally asked him what the people living there were thinking of all the noise he was creating.

In response to my question, he belligerently responded, "*They don't care*", but I knew he knew better. He then sped across town to park in a vacant lot where he left the car to sit on some wood crates. Thinking he wanted to be alone, I waited in the car and apparently dozed off. When I awakened, Mac had gotten himself a beer and the boy was now gone.

Feeling the need to lighten things up, I told him a story about how my older brother and I once went to a quiet neighborhood and poured bleach on the tires of his car, to generate huge clouds of smoke while screeching like a wild banshee! He thought that was hilarious and we both laughed and laughed!

Considering the mix of whimsical and political was a dream about another famous actor in 08 that I will call "*Rick*" and a "*door*". Rick was being asked to *install* a **blue** *door* in a blank *white* wall. The problem with installing the *blue* door was that Rick knew that to not do it would end his film career (as he has known it). He was very reluctant and tried to hold out, but finally succumbed!

I don't what was going on in that actor's life at the time, but considering Hollywood is extremely *political* (blue=left) stepping to the wrong side of the political isle was usually career suicide.

Interestingly, in my dreams (and night visions) it seems I am given a peek into both sides. The first one was my shaking hands with President Bush in 04 at the Republican national convention.

I met Mr. Bush on the platform where He had just given a speech and we shook hands, and I asked him a question, which he answered (but I didn't remember what).

Meeting President Bush in that dream was interesting considering another dream I had 4 years later. In it, I was standing in a rural place looking at two *earthen* **bridges** crossing a couple ravines while hearing people yelling "*No more Bush*". Just then I realized that the earthen bridges were somehow George Bush! (Speaking of symbolism)

Next, I heard some kind of *capitulation* occurring and then an agreement (behind the scenes) for "*no more Bush*"! Everyone was happy, but then I looked and saw that there was still another Bush!

Interestingly, George Bush lost the election in November 2008 but, Jeb. his brother was still a future contender for the presidency! Meeting Mr. Bush those *two* times was very interesting indeed, but nothing compared to the couple times I spent with his successor (in night visions)!

The first *encounter* was with a group of us leaving a meeting room in a high-rise office building, when suddenly two security guards blocked off about a dozen of us from the rest; informing them to *leave* the building. The guards ignored our protests and announced; "*The president is in the building*".

They then ushered us into a room where we waited until the President walked in! This will cost you eight dollars he announced, and we all dug in our pockets.

He then announced that some man (whose name I don't recall) would now be his full-time *assistant* and then another man (one standing next to me) would be his new *gardener.*

This dream was very interesting, but even more so when I woke up in *another* dream where I was *dreaming* and realized that it was a *dream **within** a dream*! Those have happened a few times and bring to mind an interesting movie called "*Inception*". Inception is a fascinating movie about layered dreams but sheds only little light on the whole *concept* of *dreaming* and its *origins.*

The *first* dream I had about President Barak raised some very interesting questions that left me scratching my head, but nothing compared to the *second* one that occurred in July of 2010.

This dream opened in a hotel banquet room with a glass wall overlooking the water (and pool) where what looked to be about a 50' table was being set. Just as the last of the table setting were placed, President Barak Hussein walks in with his entourage. He took a seat near the end of the table with his back to the glass. I was seated a few chairs to his right on the *opposite* side of the table.

Just then I heard someone faintly calling my name. I looked around to see if anyone had heard it, but no one seemed to, but then I heard it again. I got up and poked my head in the hallway where I saw a woman way down the hall with her head out a doorway with a phone asking if I was the one she was calling, to which I replied; "*Yes*". She then said; "*You have a phone call*".

I walked down the hall and asked *who* it was to which she replied; "*It's President Calderon, the President of Mexico*" I gushed; "*what would he want with me*"? She responded; "*I don't know*"! So I took the phone and said; "*Hello Mr. Calderon*", to which he asked; "*Who is this*"? I replied; "*Doug Huffman*" to which he responded; "*I need to speak to Mr. Obama*"!

I took the phone down to the banquet room and announced to President Barak that President *Calderon* wanted to talk to him. *Obama* looked at me and said; "*Well, I don't want to talk to him*"! I didn't know *what* to *say* or *do* (because I knew they were friends) until someone at the other end of the table began *snickering*! Then the President smiled and reached for the phone; it seems the *joke* was on me!

This chapter of celebrity dreams was, if nothing else, *entertaining* (at least for me) considering they were so real and difficult to remember as **only** *dreams* or night *visions*. But, when included with all the *other* dreams and types of dreams, it does make one *scratch* ones head as to **what** *dreaming* is **really** all *about*.

Again, we must not forget the importance the *ancients* placed upon *dreaming* and *dreams*. Obviously, they **knew** and *understood* **things** we have *dismissed* as **folklore** and *forgotten*. Where, after all, did the Native Americans *acquire* the belief that dreams do *not* come **from** our **own** *minds*?

Chapter 6

Personal Prophetic Warning Dreams

Considering the ending statement of the last chapter regarding *dreams* and *dreaming*, have we really been **gaining** *understanding* or *losing* it because of *our* **pride** in our **supposedly** *superior* modern understanding. We must keep in mind, ancient writing and archeology both **confirm** the *ancients* had "**floating** *cities*", **spacecraft** far *advanced* from ours, and even **nuclear** *weapons*! (*Ancient Aliens* and the *Mahabharata*) Considering that, did they really *understand* **less** about *dreams* than we do?

Of course, I personally do not have the luxury of dismissing the **prophetic** dreams and *visions* I have *experienced* and related in earlier chapters. Bottom line; even the so- called *experts* are *only* **guessing** as to **what** *dreams* **are** and **where** *they* **come** *from*!

In an earlier chapter, we saw how the ancients in the Biblical record put *great* **stock** in *dreams* and their *meanings*, especially as *warnings*. We saw some of those *warning* dreams, like what the *Pharaoh*, his *cupbearer* and *baker* all had.

And, if we are to believe what is recorded, it was the Pharaohs' taking the dream and its *interpretation* **seriously** that *saved Egypt* and ultimately *Joseph's* **family** as well as his *extended* family. Are such warning dreams really no longer given? Are you willing to bet on it?! Considering my *own* **experiences**; I wouldn't!

If *what* is recorded for us in **Genesis** is true, *what* has *changed?* In fact, a *well **known** axiom* uttered by George Santayana, quoted by Winston Churchill and many others states; "*those who fail to learn from history* (or don't believe it) *are doomed to repeat it*"!

It seems history is an ***unfailing*** *reality* that ***repeats*** *over* and *over* and *over!* Obviously, it's because *human **nature*** does ***not*** *change* no matter how many millennia pass!

The prophetic dreams and warnings we read earlier about the butler and baker in Pharoah's court certainly prompts the question; have those personal *prophetic* dreams and/or *warnings **stopped***, or have they only appeared to *disappear* simply because we no longer *accept* or *believe* in them?

I personally can say; yes, they are *still **given*** and *still* come to *pass.* That said, I will relate one that was *given* me and came to *fruition* with shocking precision once I understood the *symbolism* used.

It began in a castle looking out my master- bedroom window where I was surprised to see a woman and two young children getting into a small *rowboat* in the castle moat.

This woman and her two young children had no oars or push pole and she was strangely just stood in the boat looking as if she had no clue *why* she was there or *where* she was going. But, she did succeed in *crossing* the *moat* and *entering* the castle as the dream continued.

The woman crossing the moat was actually a woman I had met after a friend told me her husband had died and she needed help. I went to her house to help her with some *repair* issues, but wasn't sure if she was someone I *wanted* or *should* be *friends* with. Interestingly, that's when the *prophetic **warning** dream* came.

Obviously; with the dream so full of such interesting (and strange) *symbolism*; I couldn't help wondering about it. In doing so, a few anomalies jumped out at me leading me to consider the dream might be a warning. But, I had never had such a ***warning*** *dream*, and didn't know if I should take it seriously.

But, the night vision was rife with ***red*** *flags*, such as her crossing my *castle* ***moat*** in her little boat. That action screamed that she was ***not*** an ***invited*** *friend*. The moat is one of a castle's *defenses* that only *enemies* ***cross***; *family* and *friends* ***use*** the *drawbridge*!

Obviously, the symbolism left me wondering *how* I could *conclude* she was *a friend*. But then, I am quite fussy about the *kind* of *people* I am willing to call my *friends*.

But, her standing in the middle of the boat looking all around and drifting (across) as if she didn't have a *clue* ***where*** she was *going* was a *curious* anomaly.

That little irregularity told me that her *not* being a ***welcome*** *friend* was not *intentional* on *her* part; but to be taken seriously none-the- less. In fact, after getting into the castle, her actions (and words I didn't remember exactly later) left little doubt as to ***what*** *kind* of person she was.

To make a long story short, after a year of my being a good friend to her (doing things for her and her kids) she finally *revealed* her *dark* side when she finally took off her mask to reveal her *true* self. It turned out that she most certainly was not someone I could *trust* as a friend or would want to be friends with, we so went our *separate* ways.

True *friendship* (and being a true friend) is extremely important to me and someone who *cannot* be trusted (in the end) can *never* be a ***real*** *friend*! So, the vision was *correct* and was a ***true*** *warning*. Needless to say, I pay more attention to such dreams (night visions) now.

I would like to *relate* one more **prophetic** *warning* dream before moving on to a very striking one from a good friend that nothing less than shocking.

In this dream I had gone down to the entrance of the cul-du-sac (which I lived at the end of) with my youngest daughter and looked southwest to get a better look at a giant funnel cloud we saw come down. As we watched, we were shocked to see a black puff of smoke emerge from the funnel that seemed to be very much animated and alive!

It had a very demonic feel and I was afraid it would come down the cul-du-sac after my daughter and I, so I told her to get to my house as I hoped to lead it away to the next street to the north.

Just as I hoped, it passed our cul-du-sac moving up the major street, to the little street I was hiding on. I then ran down to the first street (which happened to be anther cul-du- sac) to see if it would follow; which it again did!

I then ran down the dead end street to the house behind mine and around it into my backyard to again watch to see if it would follow. To my relief and chagrin (for my rear neighbor) it came around the house and entered into the back of that house!

I won't elaborate except to say that I knew the person who lived in that house and that event turned out to be a *turning* point where everything in her life came *crashing* down. I felt so bad like I should have been able to something, but at the time, I wasn't even sure at time if it was real.

Winding down this chapter then, I will *relate* the extremely interesting prophetic (warning) dream a good friend of mine experienced that I alluded to earlier. It was heart breaking in one sense, but very eye-opening in light of this chapter's subject!

She was a young mother with three children; two sons and a daughter (second born) when she had a dream about her baby son. It opened on ship where there was dancing and celebrating with all the children, including her baby son, in an adjacent baby-sitting room.

Unfortunately, the ship was sinking and this young mother found it extremely *disturbing* that the other parents seemed to be acting so indifferent (like on drugs) towards their children. After making this observation, she went to get son to find that part of the ship flooded and her son gone.

She then set her mind and all her energies into her family's financial well-being, which caused her friends and family (and church) to turn *against* her and everything to go bad. In the dream she ended up losing everything, but instead found herself with a group of friends and relatives, bathed in the warmth of a bright *light* shining only on her. She then remembers being given a throne by that light!

She then remembered the light putting his hand on her shoulder and told her (and those gathered) that she would have that throne and position *forever* and *ever*. As the warm *light* was *departing* He softly spoke to her and informed her that as proof of His promise she would soon shake the hand of a certain evangelist she knew from her church!

That was the end of her dream, but not long after, she and her family found themselves at the auditorium where that particular evangelist was speaking, with a line of people waiting and hoping to shake his hand. Her dad was with her and asked her if she wanted to shake the evangelist's hand, but she said "*no*".

Because of that, the easiest way to go was around the back of the auditorium when to her surprise; out comes the evangelist! She tried to *avoid* him but he came directly to her and her family and shook **her hand!** That was the **proof** the **shining** one had *promised* her, but sadly, her son did die at age 26 of a heart attack!

Chapter 7

Progressive (farmhouse) Dreams
New Beginning

As the title of this chapter indicates, it deals with a very interesting and bizarre aspect of dreaming (and/or night visions) *"progressive dreaming"* mentioned in an earlier chapter. Again, progressive dreaming is when a dream picks up where an earlier dream left off and *continues*.

It seems to be a very *uncommon* type of dreaming which I have not *read* or *met* anyone else having (although, I'm sure I'm not the only one)! The fact that I was having (being given) these *progressive* dreams was bizarre enough but all these dreams were a part of a dream sequence that had a **common** *core* and/or *theme*; my *childhood* **farmhouse**.

Not only were these *dreams* and *night* **visions** *progressive*, but many have *proven* to be **prophetic** as well. But, to relate them all would be a book in itself, so I am putting together a few in the overall sequence, beginning with the *first* one; to show how *bizarre* and *unusual* this *progressive* dreaming was. In fact, the very first one was *prophetic* and set the stage for the rest.

Even though the farmhouse dreams were sprinkled among others, they obviously **stood** out. This *first* of these progressive farmhouse dreams then, came in December of the year 2000. I related it in an earlier chapter, so here I will just hit the high-lights to refresh our memories for the *farmhouse* dreams that *followed.*

It opened in the southeast cowyard of the farmhouse as an old *medicine* (show) *wagon* suddenly tore through the south fence in a cloud of dust and rumbled to a stop in center of the yard.

In the middle of that dirty dilapidated wagon, was a man dressed in a dark expensive looking suit! As it turns out, the man was an evangelist who was related to a friend of mine; so we decided to go see him at a service he was holding in a northwestern AZ town. Interestingly, he looked exactly as I saw him in the medicine wagon in that night vision.

As I related in an earlier chapter, a while later at a gathering of some friends, I mentioned that I had gone to this evangelists services, when suddenly a woman piped up; "*Stay away from him; he's a con man*"! As it turns out, he had defrauded an elderly couple (I knew) out of a very large sum of money!

Interestingly, this evangelist also had a night vision showing a map of Utah overlaid on a map of ancient Judea! What a coincidence that Jerusalem was called Zion and the place this evangelist founded in northwestern Arizona, southeast of "**Zion**" *Utah*! Astounding as that was, Utah is also a variation of the name "*Judah*" (Yudah)

I also shared earlier that I realized how the farmhouse and surrounding cowyards were laid out just like the ancient Israelite temples in Jerusalem and as the dreams progressed; it became obvious that the farmhouse was a representation of the Israelite Temple of Solomon! The way it all fit together was nothing short of astounding!.

In the next few farmhouse dreams I found myself *rebuilding* all the old dilapidated, falling- down farmyard buildings, and turning them into *houses* for *people*. One of the most notable was a two-story house for a couple I was good friends with. The house I built them was just northwest of where the evangelist came into the cowyard!

Interestingly, I helped find her and her daughter a new house in a little town in Southern Utah. In relationship to where it was in the dream versus reality, was exactly the same! At the time, its location and that it was two levels (like in the vision) hadn't even entered my mind. It wasn't until years later that I realized that bizarre reality! In fact, in the night vision it had a curved staircase with her daughter living on the lower level; just as it turned out in real life.

Before continuing with the rebuilding of the farm buildings, I need to set the stage by relating one of the most shocking dreams (night visions) ever. The dream opened with my older brother and I returning to the old farmhouse to find something was very *wrong*.

As we entered the farmhouse everything was bathed in an eerie *red* glow accompanied by an overwhelming **demonic** *presence* and *feel* of *evil*. I noticed a picture of a beautiful young woman on the wall which I somehow knew was not right and turned to my older brother as stated; "*things aren't always as they seem*"

To show him what I meant, I sprayed something on the picture to reveal the shocking *true* picture; that of an older woman performing a lesbian act on the young one. Even more shocking was that the older woman's breasts were the naked heads of *animals*!

There was much more to the dream (night vision) which I will share later but for now it's necessary to understand a key point of the *progressive* farmhouse dream series. Without this key understanding, the whole dream series is just nonsense! You see, the once *holy* (righteous) temple, pictured by the farmhouse, had become *evil* and *demonic*.

With that in mind, we must also understand that the United States is the largest of the *modern* Israelite tribes; *"Ephraim"* where the Tabernacle was kept in ancient times (Shiloh) for over 200 years! So for Zion (place of the temple) to be in the heart of the US makes perfect sense. It seems the farmhouse was a teaching *simulation* of the bigger picture!

Remember the dream I related earlier; my flying exodus from the farm that ended my *recurring* flying dreams from the farmhouse? It was after that flight to the *southwest* that I *returned* in a night vision to find the demonic *infestation*!

There were a couple more such *exodus* dreams; (apparently different groups of people) which are another story. But, what a shock (but understandable) to find my father (representing God (YHWH) bulldozing (leveling) the cowyards and the farmhouse in one of the ensuing farmhouse dreams!

He even allowed me drive a bulldozer! Even though I knew the farmhouse had become so evil, helping *level* it made me feel strangely *melancholy*.

Interestingly, it was after these bulldozing of the cow yards and farmhouse dreams that I began having dreams of *building* a *new* farmhouse!

About the same time, I also began *rebuilding* the *outer* farm *buildings* that *separated* the cowyards from the *inner* farm yard. One of those rebuilds was turning the old *granary* into the two-story house for my friend and her daughter that I shared earlier. I also built a mansion for a Jewish woman, which I found very interesting in its implications.

Other rebuilds' included *replacing* the old falling down barn with an *auditorium* and building a *cafeteria* where I helped prepare feasts! With helpers, I also turned the old *pig* barn, *chicken* house, and even the *well* house, into beautiful homes; a couple of which I lived in (in my dreams).

At the same time all the *rebuilding* of the *farmhouse* and *outer* buildings was happening, there were *other* things happening like *wells* being drilled in the front yard (and the north cowyard) and a *skating* rink in the *west* (back) yard. Dad also *planted* beautiful *gardens* that produced amazing fruit. For example, one garden had *wheat* stalks eight foot tall!

While laying bricks on the Farmhouse (which was two stories now) a *school* was built in the front yard where one day, I decided to join the kids for lunch. Unfortunately, I was shocked to find hundreds (if not a thousand) of kids waiting in line to eat, so I decided to eat another time.

During the reconstruction, something very surprising happened; my Father *instructed* me to *build* an *addition* on the Farmhouse for someone and his wife who were very special! It was this dream that solidified the notion that the Farmhouse was my *Spiritual* **Father's** *House*!

It was July of 03 when I had the dream of *building* the *addition* onto my Father's house (for someone *special*) in walked the *ones* for which I was building it; the *Messiah* (Yahshua) and His *betrothed*! I was so *surprised*, but interestingly, took an immediate *liking* to them both!

At this point, anyone very familiar with the Bible should be seeing some very interesting *parallels*. For instance; a couple scriptures in the NT gospels, the *Hebrew* Messiah told His *disciples* that He was going to His *Fathers'* **mansion** to *prepare* (build) a **place** for them and then come back to *get* them!

Plus, among the *parables* He told them were ones involving a *wedding supper, bridesmaids*, a *bride* and *bridegroom*. Interestingly, one of the parables was *one* where all these people were *invited* to a *wedding*, but none of those **first** *invited* came. Those that ended up *coming* were those **"outside"** the inner circle of *family* and *friends*.

In light of *that* parable and not *forgetting* the dream of building the *addition* onto the **Father's house** for His Son and bride, was another amazing and shocking dream, so very *appropriate*! In this dream I found myself in front of the farmhouse with a woman in a wedding dress standing not far away!

It seems I had been given the *responsibility* of *building* a *vehicle* to *chauffeur* her to her *wedding*. I shortly had one *prepared*, which was about ten feet tall, looking very much like two suv's stacked up! I drove this strange vehicle from the bottom cab with the woman (bride) in the top coach.

Interestingly, the wedding was to take place in the *new **banquet** hall* where the old barn was, that I helped *build* in an earlier dream.

Ushering her in, I was rather surprised to find that there were *no* guests! Not only that, *nothing* was *prepared* or *ready* for the wedding. There were many people around outside, but **none** *inside*. It was as if *no one* was *aware* (or perhaps cared) of the upcoming wedding! It was just like the parable of all the *friends* and *family* that *declined* to attend, so *average* **nonfriend** or ***family*** were brought in.

Another interesting *progressive* Farmhouse dream during this segment was that of *terrible **wind** storm*, which woke me up from my sleep in the farmhouse. (You notice that now I was living in it!) At any rate, I went out to the addition we were *building* to see if there was any *damage*.

The addition was only about *half* completed but had *doors* and *windows*. The wind had flung the doors open so hard it *broke* the *windows* next to them! The windows were very *exotic* and I was upset about having to *replace* them!

Going back into the main house, I met my Dad coming out and told Him about the broken windows, but He seemed unconcerned. Rather than going to see the damage, he took me out to *plant* some *trees* instead!

Speaking of *trees* at the Farmhouse, another dream had me standing in the west yard looking at all the trees in the cowyard just to the south. I could see that most of them were *dead*. As I watched, a woodpecker landed and began pecking for bugs, which made me realize they needed to *cut down*.

Cutting down the *dead* trees was indeed *appropriate* in light of my father taking me out to help him *plant **new** trees*. There were many other *related* dreams of the same nature, such as one standing on the back porch looking at the backyard (west) which was now very *lush* and *green*!

In this one, I was commenting to my Dad that the grass needed mowing because we were expecting company, but the problem was, it was the Sabbath and I didn't want to *dishonor* it! But, my Dad said not to worry as a lawn mower appeared and began mowing by itself! I was very surprised and was wondered if the mower could be trusted to do a good job without being directly guided?

Also, on the back side of the backyard, there was a gorgeous *garden* that my older brother had planted. I went to look at it and was amazed at how *beautiful* everything looked, and with no weeds! The vegetables were *gorgeous*!

Just then it was *dinner-time* and we all went into the house to eat. A banquet table was set up with every kind of food on it. But i had to take mine *to go* because i had to go to this little town to get some mirrors. I don't know what they were for, but one was too heavy for me to lift, which I asked them to deliver, but for some reason, they *refused*.

Then, in another one Farmhouse dream, I was helping dad cut that shockingly tall grain in the field to the northeast. It was so tall, even on the tractor I couldn't see above it! This is where things took an interesting *turn* when I cut enough grain to get a good view of the surrounding area which as far as I knew was just corn fields. It was quite a shock see what had happened!

Along the road surrounding the field and leading up to the farmhouse were all these beautiful new homes; gorgeous brick and Tudor mansions, among others! Then as we got back up to the farmhouse there was another beautiful building, a design I had never seen before, standing just on the other side of the cowyard fence east of the Farmhouse. It was very beautiful, but when i went in, I knew it was connected to, or was *built* by satan!

The next farmhouse dream found me back to work on the special *addition* to the south side of the old farmhouse. I was doing the drywall and was getting a lot done, which is unusual for these dreams. Usually i am frustrated in my dreams and can't get anything done. This dream was followed by one that included our wives, getting ready for a meal where a lively discussion about the *name* "**YHWH**", seemingly about *different* spellings and *pronunciations*. Anyway, I had a bucket of cream and decided to make it into *butter* for our dinner.

After finishing the butter churning and placing it on the table, I was shocked to see a few minutes later that the butter had caught fire along with the other food! Suddenly I realized that it was a burnt offering, but was sad that we weren't going to have any fresh sweet butter for dinner.

I then went back and looked in my pail and to my surprise, found it still half full of butter even after I had put all of it on the table!

I though how appropriate the burnt offering was considering the *finishing* of the *addition* for *Yahshua* (the Messiah) and His *bride*!

Burnt offerings were customary in ancient times to *bless* a *momentous* **occasion**; like a *wedding* or christening today, but that burnt *offering* led to a very interesting follow-up dream a couple weeks later.

It was an absolutely perfect summer day in the west cowyard of the Farm as I walked past long rows of tables of people *eating* and *drinking* endless varieties of food and drink. The tables went on for about a quarter mile into the southwest pasture. Apparently, this was *Yahshua's* **wedding** *feast*!

Another strange twist in the series was this dream of *supervising* the *construction* of a very *odd* and *interesting* building in the *south* yard where *nothing* had ever been built. Interestingly, it was being built out of **clay bricks**. I was very excited about the building because it was going to be many stories high in a *stepped* design.

After a few stories were completed, I suddenly realized that it was looking too much like the tower of Babel and limited its design to only *three* levels. After wakening, I realized it still looked like an Aztec temple! Apparently, that *bad* move was a **turning** *point* as you will see!

Not long after, I was in the west farmyard enjoying the beauty when suddenly the back door flew open and some young people came running out to meet me. This would not have been unusual except for the shock to see that one young woman was completely naked!

The naked young woman began hanging on me; obviously feeling *amorous*, but I *refused* to accommodate her, which upset her and *prompted* her *return* to the house.

Unfortunately something was *changing* in the farmhouse and *not* for the good considering that about this time a lot of *strange* animals began *appearing* at the farmhouse! That may not seem like any big deal until it's realized the **defected** *watchers* (angels) were animals!

Of these animals to appear in my dreams, there was one animal resembling a small sheep, except that it was bright *yellow, pink, red*, and *black* in color and looked like a stuffed animal with seams. It also had a head of what appeared to be a small dog!

There were a lot of other *strange* animals, which in the beginning were very *friendly* and *good,* but began taking a very *negative* (evil) turn as things went on.

One of the *good* ones was a *cow* I had brought in for milk. She had a monstrous *milk* bag and *udders* so big that took both hands to squeeze them! And shockingly, she gave some **two** *gallons* of milk from *each* udder!

During this phase of the Farmhouse dream series, everything was *growing* and *blessed* greatly, but there was a dark side *developing*. One of the dreams showing this **negative** *turn* of *events* was one next to the auditorium in the front farmyard.

It seems a huge *snake* had moved in, which suddenly sprang out from between some crates. The enormous snake was yellow with black stripes and over 6 feet long. It had a girth of at least six to eight inches and I hollered for everyone to come look. At the time, I didn't realize the *significance*, but just think Garden of Eden.

It seems some of the women were *afraid* to look and refused, but as the rest of us watched, it became obvious that the snake was after a cat. I yelled at the cat to run, which it did, but only got about five feet before the snake got it and began *swallowing* it *head* first. The cat desperately bit the snake's jaw, but it was too late.

On another note, I really knew something was wrong when I went to admire my Father's garden, only to be stunned by His having plowed it all up! But walking through it, I realized some of the plants plowed under were coming back. That was very encouraging sign to me, which prompted me to plant a garden myself next to His. In fact, another dream found me out admiring how beautiful it was doing!

In the meantime, something else happened in the farmhouse dreams, which was someone having built a *new* (second) *farmhouse* right in front of the other! That's so interesting considering in real life, my father did the same thing! Unfortunately, in all of this, something was very amiss!

The first time I dreamed of being in the new farmhouse, was walked down the stairs to the *basement*. As I neared the bottom, I found it barricaded. Just then a girl about 10 appeared to on the bottom step and look up at me.

Just then a black cat flew out of the darkness at me, which I *deflected* to unfortunately land on the girl. It began chewing her hand, but she acted as if she didn't even notice! But then, she had such an evil look about her with black *ooze*, like **black** *blood*, coming from her eyes.

Then suddenly the scene *changed* as another young girl came out of the darkness to the steps just as the entire basement erupted into a ball of intense flames; burning up all those girls dwelling (or imprisoned) in the darkness!

Among the *evil* things occurring in the *new* farmhouse were rumors (in another dream) of groups (like gangs) *recruiting* school members to participate in an armed *coup* to take *control* of the farmhouse, which they then did.

Being desperate to do *something*, I *pretended* to be one of them by *wielding* a fake (glue) gun pretending to look for prisoners to take. I then found and pointed the glue gun at two girls and ordered them to *"walk"*.

I got a break when I found an unsuspecting coup member whom I struck to get his gun. Now I had a *real* gun and really looked the part. I then marched the girls out the back door and into the *northeast* yard. Considering the coup people were taking everyone to the *southeast*, I figured we would be safe in the *northwest*.

After that dream, I found myself paving the entire north yard in concrete. I poured about one third of it the first day and for some reason I don't understand, embedded a giant ruby about a foot square and 6 inches thick, into the concrete. Then, before I could finish paving the entire yard, a flash flood rolled in from the north, washing in a boat.

I felt bad for the owner of the boat because I knew it had gotten heavily damaged as it skidded to a halt on the concrete paving. Just then, a man I didn't recognize (maybe the owner of the boat?) poked his head out.

I can't say I have a clue about the meaning of the dream meant except that the ruby is my birthstone and I was planting my presence. Plus, the concrete paving seemed to coincide with the **growing** *urbanization.* The flood showed the increasingly frequent inclement weather patterns; such as the tornado in a few dreams earlier. There were many more of those to come until the "*big one*" finally hit!

Before getting into further dreams of *urbanization* and *violent* weather, a very shocking dream helped me understand so much more about who "I" (in the dreams) was!? I had assumed I was *me* in the dreams, but that didn't always make sense until after a very *strange* dream!

When this dream opened, I was on the south side of the Farmhouse weeding Dad's garden. A young man was with me to whom I was apparently showing the ropes. The really *strange* part was the *question* he was having a great deal of trouble understanding; "*Why does YHWH place so much importance upon these little Earth creatures*"?

Knowing **our** *superiority* to them, it was hard to understand YHWH's feelings for them. In fact, the vegetables in the garden "**WERE**" *these* **humans**! Right after his asking the question, I inadvertently pulled up a watermelon plant tangled with the weeds and felt badly. I *replanted* it, but doubted it would live.

Then, seeing the sun coming up, we headed east for a very important event, which was to *occure* at **dawn**! (Interestingly, the Bible speaks of YHWH's *coming* at *dawn*"!) What a shock that dream was, but it sure brought home the fact that *things* are rarely as *we* **believe** they *are*!

With that thought, I would like to get back to *where* this dream series was *heading* and *why* with another dream involving the *encroaching evil* that seemed to be about to *engulf* the Farmhouse with a dream of driving away from the Farmhouse and having my car quit.

I then began walking through the field to a house under construction just to the south. About halfway there I noticed a *death* memorial. I went to *investigate* and discovered that the dirt around it formed ***dragonheads*** about six inches across! Again, another sign that evil was slowly *creeping* in!

I'm striving to avoid getting bogged down with too many of the dreams showing the ***moral*** *decline* of the Farmhouse and environs, but this next one had a very strange twist, which also shows the continuing urbanization around the Farm as well!

The dream opened in a mall jewelry store in a nearby town where there was a robbery in progress. I jumped in to help the store manager but there was gun fire and things were getting out of hand! But, the robbery was foiled and the robbers killed.

Then I noticed a couple girls I assumed were employees, wearing some necklaces that I knew had been stolen. I angrily yanked the necklaces off their necks and told them I was not going to *allow* them to *steal* because it was *wrong*. They seemed to be *apologetic*, but for some reason I still felt the need to bring them to the Farmhouse.

As we approached the Farmhouse from the southwest, I was astounded to see all the new houses! There was even another street coming in through the south field. We drove up the new street close to the Farmhouse to climb up on a low building to get a better look at all the new houses!

Just then *three **lightning** bolts* came down in the northeast and converged on the ground, turning bright blue and following the ground up to the farmhouse!

The sound they made was like that of a jet aircraft followed by an explosion as they struck the Farmyard! Before we could recover from our shock, *three* more struck! Then a black man with a gun scaled the west side of the building we were on causing us concern that he would shoot us until another man chasing him assured us all *under* control!

Interestingly, in a dream shortly after, I was drawing new boundaries for the southeast cowyard on a map! I'm not sure, but did that mean there was no longer room for everyone in the Farmhouse? Afterwards, I went to my brothers' house, about 3/4th of a mile east of the farmhouse.

Again I was shocked to see how many houses had been built. As far as I could see, was now endless city! But along with the exploding *growth*, more *strange* as well as *destructive* things were *happening,* like this next dream!

When this dream opened, I was with a group running across the field to the northeast of the farmhouse. It was after midnight and pitch black, except for the star shaped bombs falling all around us! We fell down on our bellies and crawled praying that the bombs would miss us.

Suddenly I felt myself being covered with insects (locusts, I think) but then they were gone and the bombing stopped as well! It was now beginning to dawn as we headed to the farmyard to celebrate our *assumed* victory!

Right after celebrating the apparent victory over the star bombing, I made an *effigy* of the *pharaoh* of Egypt and was *burning* it in front of the Farmhouse! After the burning, there was singing, dancing and lots of food in tents. Sitting at one of the long tables, I noticed two young girls kissing and fondling each other, at which point I went over to them and ordered them to leave!

The next dream was one where I came back from the southeast cowyard and found police cars surrounding it. I asked one of the agents who introduced himself as being *"from the **red** division"* (red meaning communist?) what was happing. Apparently, they had *arrested* mom and dad with charges I knew were *false*.

That dream left me feeling very discouraged and this next dream didn't help. It opened in an arena full of people. Around the walls was a row of chairs with people. Apparently everyone in the arena was there to watch a medical procedure involving the sample taking of a very *contagious* virus from some infected people that had been brought.

The next scene opened back in the farmhouse where a woman brought the same virus samples in! I was very upset about the possibility of the farmhouse being contaminated and told her to get them out of there.

What an interesting scenario considering the Ebola scare beginning in 2014 with the bringing in of infected Ebola people from Africa!

A related dream I had was in 2004 where I looked at the north cowyard to see all these Canadian houses there now! It wouldn't be so strange if not for the NAFA Treaty from the UN calling for the dissolution of the borders between the US and Canada (and Mexico)! Interestingly, the Farmhouse seems to be the heart of the US.

As the dreams continued, so did the building but now it was not so easy anymore. I was helping build another room addition on the farmhouse, but unfortunately, we were having trouble because of the now overbearing government regulation!

The crushing government regulation wasn't the only thing happening; all the while, flying overhead were fighter jets and helicopters. It had us all worried that something bad was eminent and could erupt at any moment!

But, the building went on as was the case in this dream. It was getting dark and a few of us had taken a walk to southwest of the Farmhouse and were astounded to find crews putting the finishing touches on a massive highway; at least 20 lanes wide! I was commenting as to the necessity of such a highway.

What an amazing dream considering the trans-continental (Mexican trade highways) system that was begun to be built some ten years after this dream!

Another interesting development was tossed into the mix when in another dream found me walking down to the west cowyard to see the yard surrounded with billboards announcing even *more* development!

After *leaving* and *returning* a few days later (in the dream) it was a surprise to find even more billboards but that the Chinese were constructing the buildings! The crazy thing is, we (others locals) jumped in to help. We took building material up to the east yard, prepped it, and then installed it in the building they were constructing in the west yard!

How interesting to have had this dream considering our country for a couple decades has been *selling* all kinds of *materials* to China for their *manufacturing* and then they *build* things and send them back to the US sell to us! Since, then, they have begun building manufacturing plants on our own soil!

Another dream showing further moral decline that seemed to be coming with the building boom was one where I was driving south from our farmhouse where the railroad tracks used to be (now a huge freeway). Before i knew it, I was in Mexico where I met someone who said they could show me around. I

I followed him under some bridges in a really bad part of a Mexican city where we came across a stinking rotting corpse covered with *flies* and *maggots*. But that was only the beginning! Soon, they were everywhere! Some had not been dead very long and I couldn't help but to see that they looked like *prostitutes*! It then became clear that this was where they *killed* and dumped the *hookers* when they were done with them! Some of the more recently killed ones were wearing very *expensive* clothing like high end **call** *girls*!

Another very interesting development showed up in another dream which was the discovery of oil at the farmhouse. I had gone down into the basement when my dad came in talking about digging a hole for something in the middle of the basement (dirt) floor.

So I took a pole I was carrying and stabbed it into the dirt to see if there were any soft spots to dig. To my shock, crude oil began to flow up from the place I jabbed the dirt. I did it again in two more places only to find more crude oil!

That dream occurred in 2003 and what a shock it was for massive amounts of oil to be discovered in North Dakota (heartland) and Colorado (also Texas) in shale deposits and on private land where the government couldn't stop it! Suddenly, oil prices began to drop, ending the need to *import* oil from the Middle East!

Strangely, about the same time I had a dream where I came to watch my Dad combine (harvest) the grain crop next to the farmyard. Finding it too green, He asked me to come back a couple days later to do it for Him.

But, after coming back to the field, I was shocked to see that it had *already* **been** *harvested*! I looked around trying to figure it out who did it when I noticed a pile of grain and realized that it was from dad's field. I asked the swarthy middle-eastern man there if he had done it, but he got defensive and *angry* and wouldn't talk to me; answering my question that it had been him.

It seems that since we no longer needed their oil, they began to steal our grain (food)! The parallels between reality and these dreams was (is) astounding!

Considering the declining trend, another appropriate dream showing up, was where I found myself shoulder to shoulder with hundreds of other people around the main front yard of the farm house. It seems we were expecting an enemy (goat) attack! They came as expected (from the east) but looked like sheep! (Goats in sheep's clothing?)

They circled the yard and found that there was no way through us and then turned and retreated back to the East. We all went after them and began to slaughter them. As they scattered, we followed and tracked down every single one.

That dream was certainly an encouragement, but was only a temporary abatement of the decline. In fact, I began having dreams of being a *refugee* in *bombed **out** cities* with war *everywhere*. There were missiles screaming overhead and *exploding* all around. Everything was turning into a nightmare when I had a dream of coming into the farmyard off the freeway to the west.

The skies were *dark*; churning with terrifying *inky **black** clouds*. I parked my truck and motioned to my dad who was working close by (in the garden) to come and get in the truck with me. He got in just as three monstrous category 5 funnels came down and began *destroying **everything**!*

I was praying that the funnels would miss us, and they did; we *didn't* feel a thing. Suddenly, they were gone and I got out to survey the damage. To my shock, everything was gone; the whole city that had developed around the Farmhouse, as well as the farmhouse buildings, were gone! All that was left was part of the lower level of the farmhouse!

After the horrible devastating tornado dream, I realized that there was a sprinkling of strange farmhouse dreams that seemed *out of place* and made no sense until I began to assemble all the *connecting* ones. It was then that I realized that at some point, everything had *changed* and was *different*!

One of these out of place dreams was a horrible dream at the farmhouse that came after the tornadoes had destroyed everything. There were no longer any buildings, only *destruction* and *debris*. It now seemed to be a *refugee* camp, with an overturned truck trailer and little else for shelter; not so much as an outhouse! Winter was setting in and I was distressed trying to find shelter or what little protection (for the night) for groups of people who had straggled in. Unfortunately the best I could do was a couple blankets and huddling together for warmth against the *bitter* north wind.

Everything in the Farmhouse dreams looked so different now. For instance; one dream shocked me with the view of a canyon that was now just outside the farmyard to the east.

On top of that, there were a few dreams showing an ocean (or sea) on two sides of the Farmyard (south and west) with lakes to the east and north; not to mention a river running through the farmyard to the West!

Also quite interesting, was that the farmyard was now up on a large hill or small mountain! It had been originally built on a small rise on an otherwise flat landscape.

Progressive changes continued around the Farmhouse such as the dream where I found myself being instructed by a rich man to begin cleaning up the farmyard beginning with the southeast. I began the task by collecting all the dead wood and trees and burning them. Interestingly, my older brother and sister showed up to help.

Another dream that showed a profound difference between the old and new Farmhouse opened with a few of us were doing something important in one of the old buildings (moving things in and out?) In the process, I realized our efforts (with the restoration) of the Farmyard were being sabotaged by some people hiding on a roof.

After discovering them I grabbed a piece of electrical conduit (metal pipe) and went after them. I hit one and scattered the rest. I then went after the leader; spotting him hiding around a corner about 30 yards away.

I chased him (along with his cohorts) to the middle of the southeast cowyard before catching them and assaulting one of the larger ones. I then turned my attention to the leader, which to my shock, *morphed* into a *bull!* I began to work him over with the conduit while his cohorts (who were also animals) cowered a short ways away.

This dream was rather shocking because it showed that demons spirits were now *present* in **real** *time* attempting to thwart the efforts and *progress* of *restoring* the Farmyard.

While cleaning up, a rather strange and disturbing bit of information (rumor) came; that my father had *apparently* **died**. I chalked the rumor up to *disinformation* and went back to work.

Hearing a lot of noise I looked to see a family of landscapers tearing up what used to be the road into the Farmyard and putting in *plants* and *trees!* This is where I first noticed the canyon across the east side of the farmhouse mentioned before, which apparently had something to do with the landscapers.

Peering down into the canyon, it looked to be about 100 ft deep with a river flowing through it! This is also where I first noticed that the farmyard was now raised up on a mountain! In fact, there was even a pine forest further east!

Another outstanding and rather shocking development concerning the "*new Farmhouse*" was discovering a short stone wall (about 2 feet high) wall splitting the front yard (north to south) into two parts, north and south. The north-east corner of the front yard was also sectioned off by a short wall, but flooded with waist deep water.

Being a bit in awe of the new Farmyard, I waded into the water and *looked* up to discover something even more bizarre; **two** *suns*! One was low on the horizon in the west and in a lunar eclipse, while the other was *high* in the southwestern sky!

Not only were there now **two** *suns* but a **second** *moon* just to the right of the southwestern sun. For some strange reason (if things weren't strange enough) *both* suns were supposed to be in *lunar* eclipses. So I did something beyond understanding; *I caused* the second moon to *move* over in front of the *second* sun! Don't ask me how I had the *ability* and *power* to do that, but I did!

The dream really shocked me, but now looking back objectively, I'm reminded of a prophecy in **Revelation** 22 of the *New Jerusalem*, where there was *no **longer*** any *night*! Interestingly; *two* suns (and moons) would certainly eliminate *complete* darkness or *night*.

Another amazing new development highlighting the "*new Farmhouse*" that parallels the same theme with the dream of the *two* suns, was my being asked (in another dream) to *build* walls around the farmyard with large doors. I was confused and asked someone what the point of all the doors was and why only *one* wouldn't be sufficient.

When I woke up, I realized the dream was also about the walls was about the New Jerusalem in **Revelation** 22. According to that chapter each of the doors in the walls was for a *different **tribe*** of *Israel*!

To wrap up these chapters on the Farmhouse (a whole book could be written on the Farmhouse dreams alone) I want to share just one last short one where people had begun streaming in looking for *truth* and *understanding*!

This dream reminded me very much of a movie called "*field of dreams*"!

Chapter 8

National Prophetic Dreams

After earlier looking at some rather *insightful* and *remarkable* personal *prophetic **warning** dreams*, we have to ask; are prophetic *warning* dreams (visions) only *given* in a personal context, or are there *national* ones given as well?

Well, we touched on at least some of those like the *warning* dreams given the Pharaoh that were taken seriously and consequently *saved* both ancient *Egypt* and Jacob's *family* (ancient Israel).

Interestingly, there is such a *prophetic* night vision *warning* in the Bible that is playing out exactly *as **given*** right before our eyes in ***real** time*; that is for anyone *willing* to *acknowledge* and *look*! What I'm referring to *begins* with a *prophetic* vision (dream) given to the Babylonian king Nebuchadnezzar in the second chapter of the book of Daniel in Bible.

There, Nebuchadnezzar had a *night **vision*** (dream) he could ***not** remember*, which was causing him severe *consternation*. He told his *wise* men to tell him *what* the dream *meant*; and oh yeah; ***what*** the *dream **was*** as well; you see, he ***couldn't*** remember it! He informed his *seers* and *magicians* that if they *failed* to *accommodate* him, they would be *cut* to *pieces* and their houses *reduced* to *ash* heaps. (Dan.2:5-9)

Being *unable* to fulfill the kings' wishes, the *slaughtering* of the *wise* men (and their families) began until those left finally approached Daniel and his friends (captive Jews from Jerusalem) out of shear *desperation*.

Daniel told his friends to have *no* fear, that he could *do what* the king *demanded* if he would give him some time. The king *relented* and gave them a *day* for Daniel and his friends to *fast* and *pray* to YHWH (original Name for God) for the *answer*, which they amazingly received.

Here in **Daniel** 2:19, is where Daniel was given the dream and its meaning by His God YHWH

*Then Daniel went to his house and made the decision known to Hananiah, Mishael, and Azariah, his companions, that they might seek mercies from the God of Heaven concerning this secret, so that Daniel and his companions might not perish with the rest of the wise men of Babylon. Then the secret was revealed to Daniel in a **night vision**.* (Dream) *So Daniel blessed the God of Heaven.*

Interestingly, we find here Bible proof (if you accept the Bible) that dreams (night visions) do come from **outside** sources at least *some* of the time! The night vision (Nebuchadnezzar's dream and its meaning) was given by YHWH; he did not *dream* it up himself (pun intended) it was "*given*" to him! Of course, it still doesn't prove that that the Native Americans weren't *right* either; that "**all**" dreams come *from **outside*** of *us*!

Getting back to the night vision the King had, Daniel shares it with him in **Daniel**; versus 26-33 of chapter 2. There the king answered and said to Daniel, whose *slave* name given by the Babylonians was Belteshazzar;

"Are you able to make known to me the dream which I have seen, and its interpretation? "Daniel answered in the presence of the king and said; "The secret which the king has demanded, the wise men, the astrologers, the magicians, and the soothsayers cannot declare to the king. But there is a God in heaven who reveals secrets and He has made known to King Nebuchadnezzar what will be in the latter days. Your dream and the visions of your head your bed were these;

v.31 *"You O king were watching and behold, a great image! This great image whose splendor was excellent, stood before you; and its form was* awesome (huge). *The image's head was of fine gold; its chest and arms of silver; its belly and thighs of bronze; its legs of iron; its feet partly of iron and partly of clay."*

Daniel goes on to explain in the next verses that four *different* metals of the statue are *four **successive** world **dominating** kingdoms* with Nebuchadnezzar's Babylonian kingdom being the *head* of *gold*. Each *successive* kingdom would be of *lesser* quality but of *greater* strength (each metal *harder* than the one before).

History bears out that the Persian Empire (Darius the great) was the *silver* empire that *conquered* the **golden** *kingdom* of *Babylon*, who in turn was *conquered* by the *bronze* empire; *Greece* (through *Alexander* the *Great*).

Greece was then *conquered* and split into 4 parts by the *iron empire* **Rome**, with the *two iron legs* *depicting* the Roman Empire being *split* between *Rome* in the *west* and *Byzantium* (Constantinople) in the *east*.

That was an incredibly interesting *prophetic* vision of four *world-ruling* kingdoms which *came **to** pass* with amazing *accuracy* but it was Daniel's vision (dream) of the **next** *four kingdoms* that is even more astounding considering they are **still** in the *process* of **rising** and **falling**! We find them *prophesied* in **Daniel** 7; verses 1-

"In the first year of Belshazzar (Nebuchadnezzar's grandson) *king of Babylon, Daniel had a dream and visions of his head while on his bed. Then he wrote down the **dream**, telling the main facts. Daniel spoke saying; "I saw in my vision by night and behold, the four winds of heaven were stirring up the Great Sea. And **four great beasts came up** from the sea, each different from the other.*

*The first was like a **lion** and had **eagle's wings**. I watched till its* (eagle) *wings were plucked off; and it was lifted up from the Earth and made to **stand** on **two feet** like a **man** and had a man's heart given to it.*

This vision, given some 2500 years ago, is beyond shocking when **examined** *closely* in light of our current modern world! You see, most of our modern nations, curiously have a *national **animal** mascot* they *identify* with.

That is an amazing reality that jumps out in that vision of Daniel's. It's obvious by the context of that the "*beasts*" are *representative* of *nations* and/or *kingdoms*.

That in mind, how fascinating to notice *what* the ***first*** *beast* kingdom to *arise* after the *final **death*** of the Roman Empire was; that is, in light of our ***current*** *world*.

To set the context, we first need to establish the *ending* of the Roman Empire, which was the *last* of the *four* kingdoms prophesied in **Daniel** 2. Many say it was in the 5th century CE while others make the case it wasn't until the 15th century CE. Regardless, there is **no** *debating* who the *next* world *dominating* empire after Rome was. In fact, this next world empire is the *first* in history to boast of being so large that *the sun **never sets** on it*; a well known maxim!

Of course, most everyone knows that empire is the British Empire. Interestingly though, we find the *most **common** emblem* in Britain to be *the **lion***! It is found on the *Royal Coat of Arms*, the *Royal Banner of Britain* and virtually every major *family **crest**!* There are even *massive **Lion** statues* found in the famous *Trafalgar Square* in *London*. There can be ***no** denying* the **Lion** is *England's* primary *mascot!*

We also see, with a little looking, that the *eagle* is represented to a somewhat lesser degree on English *crests* in the United Kingdom as well, although not nearly as *prevalent* as the *lion*. That said; how amazing to note in Daniel's dream; a lion with eagles' wings would be the next world dominating kingdom to arise *after* the glory of the *iron* Roman Empire faded.

After a couple false starts with *Spain* and *France* almost gaining that honor, the next **world** *dominating* power was *Great Britain*, the *Lion* with **eagles'** *wings* who came out on top. Even more amazing was to see the eagle's wings get *plucked* off and lifted up to form another world dominating power; the *United States*! After all, there is no doubt the Eagle is the *mascot* of the US! We see it *everywhere* we look, even on *our* **money**!

That said, the prophetic vision of the lion kingdom getting its wings plucked to form a co-dominate kingdom (US) the *two* were lifted up to a *third* phase; one like a *man* standing on two *feet*, which is to say this first beast kingdom was divided into *three* parts; Great Britain, the United States and Israel! We must understand, it was Britain (Lord James Arthur Balfour) and President Truman of the US (and a few others) who were primarily *responsible* for *reestablishing* the *Jewish* state (modern Israel) in Palestine.

Even more interesting is to learn that Israel's mascot (the last part of the three to be formed) is a male *toddler* (Baby Bamba) Remember the *lion* and *eagle* were "*raised up to stand on two feet* (think toddler) *like a man*" (the Bamba toddler)! How more amazingly *perfect* could Daniel's vision have possibly been?

Well, the second beast kingdom prophecy by Daniel in his night vision was a "*bear*"; this is where things get really interesting. Let's look beginning in verse 5 of **Daniel** 7;

"And suddenly another beast; a second like a bear. It was raised up on one side and had three ribs in its mouth between its teeth. And they said thus to it; "Arise, devour much flesh!"

In light of that prophetic dream, how astonishing to watch that Daniel 7 prophecy play out in *real* time when in 2013, President Obama drew his red line in sand regarding *Syrian* President *Assad's* potential use of *chemical* weapons. Well, Assad *ignored* the **red** line and Obama just drew *another*! Well, to make a long story short; in the spring of 2014 Obama decided he (the US) wasn't up to solving the dilemma and turned the whole *affair* over to *Russian* **president's** *Vladimir Putin*!

Shockingly, I never heard a single news person or *talking head* say a single word about *what* had just *happened*!? What Obama had really done is *hand* the *reins* of **world** power to *Russia* (the bear)! He was admitting that the US no longer *possessed* the **power** or **authority** to *resolve* the problem with Syrian president Assad!

With Russia and Daniel's prophecy in mind, is there anyone (in the know) who doesn't understand that Russia is the *great* **bear**? In fact, the news magazines virtually *always* depict *Russia* as a huge *bear*! In fact; Medvedev, the Russian prime minister (and third president of Russia) actually means "*bear*"! How interesting the way that links *Russia* to Daniels' prophetic dream!

Of course, ever since Putin was handed the reins of world power by Obama, he began restoring the Russian Empire; taking back country after country beginning with Crimea and Ukraine! After all, who's going to *stop* him; not the US!

With the bear (Russia) on the move, is there anyone who has the *will*, let alone the *power* stop him? Even Obama himself made an offhand joke one day after leaving the white house (summer of 1014) to go golfing; "*The Bear is loose*"! Hello??

In consideration of Daniel's *world* **ruling** prophecy of the *bear* with *three* **ribs** in its mouth, we can only guess who they are. The most *plausible* case to be made is the *three ribs* are the *three* **parts** of *lion* kingdom; *Britain*, *US* and *Israel*. Another is that the *three* **ribs** are three *Balkan* countries like *Ukraine*. But, only time will tell for sure!

Again, what a shock to see prophecy given 2500 years ago, coming to *real-time* fulfillment right *before* our eyes! Bottom line and the *point* of this *narrative*; it would be very wise of us to be pay **close** attention to *dreams* and *night visions*, because we just never know where *they* are coming **from**!

After touching on the "*beast* (animal) *kingdoms*", it only seems appropriate to share some very amazing and interesting dreams; those involving Native American Indians (and animals)! These are quite interesting considering all the *Bible* dreams (and visions) we have looked at earlier involving *animals*!

Remember, the Native Americans not only believed their "*Spirit Guides*" (from the other side of the dimensional veil) were *animals*, but that one of the ways they *communicated* was *with* **dreams** (and visions)! Who knows *what* real relevance or meaning they may have, but they are rather entertaining!

Chapter 9

Indian Dreams and Visions

I'm not sure what these (some very bizarre) Native American Indian dreams have to do with me, but there is obviously something. I have never given the Native Americans much thought, so it's hard to find or see an obvious connection. Although, I suspect it has to do with my discovery of the *trans-dimensional **animals*** and *dream **weavers***!

Again, I am convinced that the *easiest* way for those on the other side of the dimensional veil to *communicate* with us is our *conscience **mind*** is *altered* or *asleep*. In fact, the Native Americans used *peyote* and *other **hallucinogens*** to *open* a *door* of **communication** (channel) with these *creatures* (animal Spirit guides) Sometimes, they were even *allowed* to *see **through*** the *eyes* of wolves or eagles in real time!

To begin my Native American dreams, I will share a rather *benign* but *strange* dream, non-the-less. It began with my leaving my grandson to see his father who apparently lived on some type of Indian *reservation*. For some reason, I knew I had to talk to him.

As I came over a rise in the reservation, I was pleasantly surprised to see the variety of wild *animal* life in the valley. It looked very much like the Serengeti in Africa!

Just then a raging bull came tearing up behind me, but upon seeing a giraffe in the valley below, turned in fear and ran the other way!

I don't know why I was being so silly, but I called him a weenie and proceeded down into the valley where the giraffe, upon seeing me, turned and ran, as I knew it would.

As the animals separated to let me through, I met this Native American man whom I assumed to be the boy's father and we walked to what appeared to be a coffee shop. It was a nice little place with a swimming pool, even.

Inside were Indians sitting around shooting the breeze in what seemed to be something like a clubhouse room? Upon my entering, they fell *silent* and stared, but I could feel them *asking* what I was doing in *"their" place*!

I have no clue what this dream was about but there were a few interesting anomalies. In the dream, I had a grandson. Well, that was 10 years before I actually did! And, although his father is not Native American, he is a dark Filipino.

Plus, why did the bull *hate* and want to *gore* me while being *afraid* of a *giraffe*? But then, I did have a bull try to *gore* me at least *three* times in real life when I was young! The strangest thing of all was the feeling that the Indians had **no** *choice* but to accept me into their circle! I got the feeling a **higher** *authority* was *commanding* them!

Speaking of bulls, it is interesting how often *bulls* have *popped* **up** in my dreams. The first time was when I went out (of the farmhouse) to feed the cows and found a huge black bull and white bull in the cowyard I needed to go into! Needing to *feed* the cows, I carefully crept in only, to my chagrin, was *attacked* by the huge *black* bull! But, to my *delight*, the *white* one came to my rescue!

That dream seemed to show that there are both *good* and **evil** *bulls* in that *spirit* world! Rather makes one wonder which ones can be *trusted* to *advise* or *protect* in the Native American relationship?

A related but very whimsical bull dream found me standing in a small western looking town and to my amazement, see cowboys driving a herd of huge (at least 7 foot tall at the back) cattle. The really shocking part was that the cowboys were *riding **bulls*** instead of *horses*; huge *bulls* with long *curly* hair!

That last dream was definitely a turning point in my bull dreams considering this next *bull* dream found me in the southeast cowyard herding a *massive* black bull into a pen in a small barn. Almost in, he got spooked and ran, but I got him back. Then I heard someone telling my dad and some others with him that **no one** had ever herded in such a *huge* bull!

It was interesting to see in that last dream how I seemed to be getting the upper hand on the black bulls that wanted to do me in. But this next one clinches it! In that one, I was getting into a yellow VW to leave the farm when I noticed a big black bull standing by the edge of the yard.

Just then my dad, yelled for me to put the bull in the cowyard before I left so it didn't follow me out. My older brother was with me and I told him, "*watch me handle that bull*"! So I went over and grabbed it by the head and *flipped* it on its back! When the bull got back up, it surprised me by saying, "*I wouldn't try to leave if your dad was leaving*"! It seemed in his mind, it was *him* or my *dad*!

Before getting back to more Native American dreams, I have to share one last hilarious (and bizarre) bull dream. It seems a guy I was riding with had just gotten a new car and wanted to see what it could do.

The guy floored the car and had it up to 110 when we saw a tractor coming at us in our lane. He swerved around it and then came to a screeching halt on the shoulder next to a cow and her calf that were behind a pasture fence.

As he got out of the car I suddenly realized he had turned into a black bull; the same breed of the cow with the calf! He was desperately trying to get over the barbed-wire fence when he got all tangled up! We thought we were going to die laughing!

Not to deviate from the topic, but earlier in the Progressive (farmhouse) dream chapter, I briefly alluded to a portion of one of the strangest and most powerful dreams I have ever had! In it my older brother and I returned to the old farmhouse to find that something was very wrong.

I could feel the overwhelming presence of *demons* and every kind of evil. I remember telling my older brother that *"things aren't as they seem"*! There was a picture hanging on the wall of this beautiful young woman which I somehow knew was a fake!

I had this spray can that I sprayed the picture with, which allowed me to see the *real* picture; to our shock, it was an older woman performing a lesbian act on the younger one.

Adding even more shock was to see that the older woman's breasts were the furless heads of animals! My bother then freaked and ran out into the pitch- black night.

I ran out after him but it was too dark to see anything. While contemplating where he might have gone, I suddenly felt a very strange sensation with my arms. What a shock to look and see my arms were actually massive black wings some 16' long! It seems I had either turned into a giant eagle or was literally in the head of *one* like the Native Americans would *experience*!

I *raised* and pushed *down* my wings and felt myself *lift* off the ground. I kept going and realized suddenly that I also had night vision! It was like a clear night with a very bright full moon. Flying higher, I could now see my brother in the middle of field running to the northeast. The bigger surprise was to see someone else *running* the *opposite* direction!

I circled and flew down close to see that it was a Native American Indian man dressed in modern clothes. As I flew down beside him, I thought it would scare him half to death, but it didn't seem to faze him! Finally he stopped and turned to me and I asked; *"Aren't you afraid of me"*; to which he replied; *"I know who are"*!

I then asked him where he was going, and he said *"to the coast"*. Then he asked me why I wasn't flying over the gulf? (That was where I flew to when I escaped from the farm years ago).

That ended a dream that I will vividly remember for the rest of my life! But, it opened the door for me to understand so many things about human interaction with a ***spirit*** *world* (on the other side of the veil) a world filled with *spirit* **animals**!

To this day, I have no idea what that dream (night vision) was really all about, except to say years later I happened to meet a young Indian girl who told me that her tribe (the Pomo's) had migrated from the Midwest (where there Eagle vision occurred) to the Pacific coast (northern Cal.) which interestingly, was what where the Indian man told me he was going!

Another seeming connected dream was one where we were tearing down (off) all the additions that had been added to the farmhouse. In doing so we uncovered a cardboard cut-out of a Native American. Shockingly, it came to life and he began helping us with the demolition of the Farmhouse additions! Again, I don't know exactly what it means but the *implications* are quite major!

With the idea of Native Americans pitching in to help, is this very interesting dream involving the little Pomo girl I had befriended. The dream involved a job (building) I was trying finish, with only the hardwood flooring and the walkways left. My crew was having trouble getting things done so I hired on a middle teen (related to Crystal, the Pomo girl) and his friends to help.

Although he didn't look Indian (American) he had a few Native Indians with him. I left and upon my return things were "*less*" done than when I had left. In fact, my original crew was gone and only the young man and "*his*" *crew* were still there.

I was a little upset and reprimanded everyone as I again left. When I returned the second time, I noticed everyone was out back eating hotdogs and hamburgers and parting!

When I inspected the project; to my surprise, everything was done and it looked perfect! But, one thing stood out in particular; the hardwood flooring that my crew had been installing from *front* to *back*, was now *left* to *right*!

A strange little aside in this dream was the date; it was 11-1-11! I'm not sure if it means anything, but it certainly stood out!

The theme of Native Americans invading my life in my dreams was not an isolated incident. There were quite a few such as one in the northern end of Main Street in Groton the town I grew up in (by). There was a small Indian tribe; half standing on one side of the street and half on the other.

The odd thing was that it was like a black and white photo with all of them dressed in traditional dress, but a young woman and her child (on the west side) stood out in full color. The photo was not close up, but I'm pretty sure the young woman and her child were the Pomo girl and her son.

At this point, I would like to reiterate my belief that these dreams are not coming from me but from the trans-dimensional dream-weavers on the other side of the veil. And with that belief, I have no doubt there is a theme and message wrapped up in all these Native American dreams.

Putting them all together, it seems there is something I do for them, such as *freeing* them in some way, to which they feel *indebted*.

This next little dream snippet shows what I mean. I looked down the hallway in my house to see two Indian braves dressed in leathers and mummified in cellophane. I got a knife and cut them free and they ran out.

In that same theme, I found myself rowing a small boat across a channel when I suddenly saw some Native Americans swimming under the water. My first thought was that I was interrupting their swim ritual and was in trouble. After seem them, I began rowing very fast but to my chagrin, they stayed right behind me.

Afterwards, it dawned on me they were not following me to hurt me but to join with me and help! This next dream brings out that conclusion.

I had just returned to my house, which was in a bad state of disrepair and went into the back yard where I was accosted by an Indian who was upset with a rat poisoning apparatus.

I told him it wasn't for rats, but mice and I didn't remember even buying it. Then I went into the house to find some Indians had moved in while I was gone. One young man had caught a wild coyote that attacked me.

That last dream, just like the first dream of this chapter, showed that for some reason, the Native Americans and I get together for some common reason. Apparently that reason involves bringing back some of their ancient beliefs as this next dream shows.

This was a vision of a woman re-dressing what appeared to be two Indian statues. She was borrowing some things from two other Indian statues. No doubt, this vision was about *reclaiming* (redressing with) *lost* ancient beliefs!

I would like to end this chapter with a couple very bizarre dreams (night visions) that tie into the Native Americans' belief systems about *shape-shifting* **supernatural** *animals* (spirit guides). In the first one, I woke up in the middle of the night to the shocking realization that a she-wolf (it looked like Koda; my wolf-shepherd mix) was standing over me in bed.

I grabbed it and forced it down where it *transformed* into a human with a cat's head and then into a beautiful young woman! Just to see if she was real, I pinched her and she hollered "*oww*"! Then I kissed her and she disappeared.

In this even stranger dream yet, I went to the northeast barn (at the farmhouse) to find an *animal* I thought was a colt locked in there. (It had a horses' head) He lying in the corner and so thin; apparently starving. I told him I was going to let him out and he stood up, but, what a shock to see a humanoid body with wings coming out of his sides!

He then raised his dirty, unkempt, and scraggly wings to touch the tips above his head. Feeling very sorry for him I walked outside to find something to help. There I found a small pen, which had not been grazed (lots of lush grass) and also a plate of chocolate chip cookies. Seeing them, I instantly knew he would love them and feel better.

Chapter 10

Out of My Head!

This chapter involves the most bizarre aspect of dreaming yet. In fact, these are the dreams (night visions) that convinced me beyond a shadow-of-a- doubt that *dreams* do ***not*** all come from us. I now have had all doubts that the Native American's were correct in their ***dream-catcher*** *concept*; that dreams *come **from** outside*!

This is such a strange *reality* it even caught the ***military's*** *attention* in the 1960's. They made a valiant effort to develop it, but apparently to no avail. They called it "*remote viewing*" and even made a star studded movie including such big names as *George Clooney*! The movie was done almost as a spoof, but I personally can vouch for the *reality* of the *concept*!

I don't know about others, but I have always wondered about all the *strange* people and *places* I would *see* and *interact* with in my dreams. These dreams (night-visions) had me scratching my head as to how our own minds could conger up all the strange faces and places I would see. It wasn't until I had a couple dreams (very detailed night visions) where I looked into a mirror and was shocked at what I saw!

The first of these I remember was getting ready to go out after waking up. I was in a small sparsely furnished house I didn't recognize, but yet was strangely familiar. After dressing, I went to a small sink on the wall by the front door to wash my face and comb my hair.

What a shock to see the face looking back at me from the mirror was a 30's something Mongolian looking man! I, on the other hand, was a middle aged Caucasian (Scandinavian-German) man.

Going outside, I was confronted with a town I didn't recognize (but yet somehow did) with machine-gun toting soldiers patrolling the streets!

That dream (night vision) was such a shock; it made me begin to look at dreams (night visions) in a whole new light. I still didn't know what to think even after having more such bizarre night visions.

In another one, a large group of us had packed our bags and were walking to a place about a half mile away where we were going to be picked up by a bus or something. About half way there, I remember I had forgotten something in the house and ran back to get it.

On the way back out, I stopped at a mirror on the wall and again was shocked to see a slim young, early 20's man! He was over 6' (I'm short and stocky) with thick curly black hair while mine was brown and graying. Again, what a shock; it felt like me, but someone else at the same time; as if I were **two** *people* at *once*!

It wasn't until I had these supposed dreams (night visions) confirmed by a few *friends*, that it finally all came together. How very coincidental that it was about that same time the George Clooney movie; "*Men Who Stare at Goats*" came out! (A lousy movie in my opinion but very enlightening)

Before that, I had one of these strange night visions where I saw a friend of mine sitting at her little desk in her house with big stacks of boxes all around and looking very overwhelmed. So, after waking up, I called her and asked to *describe* her *situation* and *feelings*. To my amazement, it was *exactly* as I saw it!

Sometime afterwards, I had another one of those night visions. It is interesting that when I have them, everything is a little gray and not in sharp focus while most of my dreams and night visions are very *sharp* and in full *color*!

Anyway, I was driving a small Japanese model car and had pulled into the parking lot of a restaurant chain where I often had breakfast. As I pulled in, I had to swerve hard to avoid a head-on collision with another car.

Thankfully we missed each other, but for some reason, I knew this had something to do with a young waitress who worked at one of those restaurants.

The next chance I had to see the young waitress, I asked her about dreaming and she confirmed she was a vivid dreamer like me. I then told her about the dream (night vision) I had that seemed to have something to do with her.

She was so shocked her jaw almost hit the floor. As she regained her composure, she gushed; "*That's exactly what happened to my boyfriend*"! I also was shocked and added; "*It happened at a different restaurant* (of the same chain) *didn't it*"? Again, she said; "*yes*"! I also told her the *type* and *color* car, which she also confirmed!

I never did see her again, but hopefully, my telling her about the vision wasn't the cause?!

What a shocking conformation that was, but it wasn't the last! I had another with the young Pomo (Indian) girl (mentioned in the last chapter) I had become friends with her at a connivance store where she worked and I would always stop for coffee.

Well, in this night vision, I was sitting in a chair overlooking a sunken living room with a rail around it, when this young woman (from the convenience store) came into the room. Judging by the lap I was looking at, I was a slightly overweight middle aged woman and the young woman was my daughter!

I had a new pair of blue jeans on my lap and told the girl I had bought them for her and to go try them on. She took them and came back looking very happy at how well they fit and looked on her.

She then went over to the rail and I had to admit they were a perfect fit and the design on the back pockets was very distinctive and nice.

I was curious after that night vision and was anxious to see and ask the young woman if she had gotten some new jeans from her mother. I didn't see her for a couple weeks, but when I did, she was busy behind the counter with her back to me and to my amazement, was wearing the very jeans I saw in the night vision!

Unfortunately, I wasn't able to talk to her and never saw her again either. It seems the place had come under new ownership and the new owners laid her off.

As amazing as those last few night visions were, they weren't the last such incidents (vision) I had and got confirmed. In yet another, I found myself in the head of a young man (strong built and over 6') who was married to another young woman who worked at a different convenience store than the little Indian girl.

Unfortunately, what I saw (experienced) was very personal and I dared not even ask the young woman about it, but a few weeks after, she introduced me to her husband (whom I had never met outside the vision) and sure enough, it was his head I had found myself in!

You see, what the military had dubbed *"remote viewing"* (verified by the movie; Men who stare at goats) was what I was experiencing. For some reason, someone from an **alternate** *dimension* has the *ability* and *reason* to link my (and apparently many others) consciousness to other people in real time! And apparently, the easiest time for them to do this is while we are sleeping.

I would like to end this chapter with an extremely bizarre and disturbing, but related dream, where I found myself in somebody else's skin; literally! Not only did I feel like I was someone else, but it seems that I had literally taken the skin off this woman and tried it on! At that point in the dream, I realized that it was wrong to take someone else's skin and I put it back on her and stitched her up!

Chapter 11

Out of This World Dreams

Considering the "*remote viewing dreams*" of the last chapter, this next chapter of dreams gives a whole **new world** to the meaning of **remote** *viewing*! Excuse the pun, but this chapter deals with *dreams* and night *visions* that occur on *other* **planets** or maybe even **other** *universes*!

The very *first* of these occurred around 2002. In the dream, a woman and her late 30's autistic daughter were traveling somewhere with me when we stopped to spend the night in a motel. The room was large with a bed in opposite corners; one they took and me the other.

I was just dozing off when I was awakened by the mother *leaving* without a word. I proceeded to doze off again when again I was awakened by the autistic daughter who had come over by my bed and was resting her head on the edge.

I don't know what happened, but the next scene found us (the daughter and I) driving through the countryside on, get this; on a *different* **planet**! Suddenly, the woman told me to pull over and she got out. She then raised her arms to the sky and *black* fluid (apparently ink) spewed out of her palms and began to form words across the sky! Unfortunately, the dream (night vision) ended before I could read what she was writing.

This next other-worldly dream found me in a strange mountainous place, where a group of us were talking about going up to the mountainside observation seats to view the moving of the dinosaur from one valley to another!

For me, it sounded *boring* and I said; *"I've seen it before"*. I then commented that *Eric Clapton could not keep it going*. I have no clue what Eric Clapton had to do with anything, but of one thing I was certain, that *place* was **not** *on* Earth!

It was interesting to hear Eric Clapton's name in that last other-worldly', but there were more such as one starring Melissa Manchester. It seems she and another 60's era woman, were hired to put on a show for some event in a strange mountain setting.

There was a lodge type building in the hills (very dry place) with a patio containing a half dozen tables set with *named* place settings. But, it seemed rather strange that for such big names, there were only a half dozen people that turned out for this dinner concert!?

The really strange thing was the way the women approached the lodge! Melissa was sitting cross- legged on a huge ***eagles*** *nest* built on top of a horse playing her guitar! The horses seemed to know what to do and walked around the building on their own as the women played! The strange feeling was that wherever this was, it was not on Earth!

Another strange dream that seemed to link two worlds (dimensions) together was one with my wife and I driving along a coast in the rain. Suddenly, the second car in front of us lost control, spun out, and was broad-sided by the car in front of us and both went over the cliff into the ocean!

When we arrived at a small hotel (motel) I told them about the accident and it struck me that no one seemed to care. Apparently, there was a play about to start in a small theater, so I went in to watch.

I sat down in one of the stepped rows which were mostly full. A man in the row ahead turned and said something about a bet amount, which made me realize that they were betting on whatever they were about to watch.

I then got up and moved to one end as a young boy opened the curtain. I was shocked to see a replay (or real time) of the accident I witnessed on the coast highway! It seems that is what these people (beings) were wagering on! Apparently we had somehow stepped behind the dimensional curtain to be able to watch things from the other side!

This next other-world dream was one of the strangest of all. In it I was leading a band of refugees (hundreds) to a new place to live. It was a place that was once inhabited, but was now abandoned, but *guarded* by a *huge* **bear** and **dragon**!

As we got close, the *bear* came after me, but considering I was a *male* **African** *lion*, I was able to run up a huge dead tree to get away. The bear and dragon finally left and I was able to lead my band through a mountain pass to a once farmed valley.

Everyone went to working the soil (with the farm equipment that had been left) and got it ready to plant. I instructed a young woman in the mixing of a white paste fertilizer and seed with which we planted the field.

In yet another other-worldly dream, I was walking through a strange semi-tropical wilderness when I glimpsed a really strange animal run over the ridge. I tried to follow it to get a better look but came to a huge river.

On the bank of the river was a fish (like a carp) that was the *size* of **whale**! I went to the river's edge and could see many more swimming under the water. Going back to where I was staying, I found my wife and daughters, and told them to come see the *monster* fish! They started to follow me but got distracted and didn't follow. Again, it was an unfamiliar planet!

Interestingly, this next night vision actually was on a familiar planet, but not Earth! It took place on Mars where a group of colonists had built a thriving community by themselves. There was a woman with a tall son about 18, who was carrying a carved out log (like a boat).

Apparently they were leaving to go live off colony. The people were worried and upset as something like this had never been done before. The really strange thing was, Mars had become lush and green with trees and streams as apparently as it had been in the distant past!

Another other-worldly dream found me in a city somewhere with church people in a glass building. There was one room in the glass building where the powers of physics were multiplied. This certainly wasn't Earth either!

One last dream that wasn't on this planet was one where I found myself on the third floor of a huge mansion so large that people on one side had never even seen the other!

The really bizarre thing was that we were preparing for liftoff! The mansion was literally a huge *flying* ship!

Chapter 12

Curiouser and Curiouser

Anyone who has see the Walt Disney Movie; Alice and Wonderland, probably remembers Alice commenting in wonder; "Curiouser and curiouser". Well, my experiences in dreaming, frequently brings her comment to mind!

Many of my dreams and night visions are just so bizarre, I don't know what to think except to write them down. And, if nothing else, they do make rather good entertainment to read! So, that is the content of this chapter; stranger than strange dreams and night visions!

This first one really had me scratching my head because it seemed so real and personal. In it I found myself observing a rolling grassy countryside with a short concrete barrier (a concrete pylon wall section being set in place) and someone behind me asked me; *"What would you say if you were given a "golden goose"?*

I didn't know what to say, and the voice then asked; *"What if we gave it to someone else"?* Again, I didn't know what to say, which ended the dream! Just exactly how does a person respond to being asked such a question? I guess I would just say *"Thank you"*!

In this next one, I was looking at a newspaper article about a black woman (and a group with her) when it came alive like a video! I was very surprised and took it to show it to a woman I knew and found her with two men.

I had taken the talking newspaper article to show a woman and found her with two men standing close by. But before I could show her, she began telling me about one of them (in a reserved but positive way) and then cut her sentence short with; "but you---" as she pulled a gun and shot at me!

Fortunately she missed, and I realized it was a man behind me she shot! I have no idea who he was and why she shot him. That was where the dream ended.

The bizarre level of my dreams and night visions really did go from one extreme to the other like this very morbid night vision. My wife and I were somewhere by water that I didn't recognize, where we decided to go for a swim. But, what a a shock to dive under the water and see dead bodies lying on the bottom.

I didn't count, but there seemed to be about a half dozen lying on the bottom; all appearing to be women! Strangely, a couple days after this dream, I called my (x) wife and told her about it. How interesting to hear that she had recently watched a movie where four women had been murdered and sunk to the bottom of a lake!

This next one opened in some strange city where I was driving around looking for a certain picture. Apparently, I was a photographer looking for the perfect shot (photograph) for a newspaper. Just then I spotted it; a 6" pipe protruding from an embankment.

As I walked over to what looked like a construction area to get the shot, a gaggle of hard-hatted people emerged from a construction trailer with a red-haired woman yelling for me to be arrested. I asked "*why*" but no one could give me an answer and they finally let me go (without my picture).

Apparently there was some sort of corruption going on which I have no clue of, but was really interesting was the shock I received next morning (in real life) to see the very same picture and incident in a comic strip!

I was in Fountain Valley California staying with my daughter when I woke up from this next dream where I had met a young woman. She was doing something with her hands which I couldn't see, but I was amazed with the length and thickness of her eyelashes! I was wondering if they were real or fake.

It was a very short and seemingly nothing dream until the morning when we went to breakfast on the pier. There I was shocked and amazed to see the same young woman sitting in another booth eating breakfast with her family! And yes, her eyelashes were quite amazing!

In this dream, I had volunteered to help a woman taking a bus full of kids to the lake. There was another woman helping her (a friend or relative) named Lisa who I sat next to. She seemed very sad and laid her head on my shoulder. Then she told me she couldn't have a relationship because she was already involved in one.

As it turns out, Lisa the woman in my vision was a housekeeper at the motel in Springdale where I was staying!

So after the dream, I decided to talk to her about it. She told me her sob story about her man and that she was in financial straits because of him. So I gave her a little financial help and left.

Waking up With Tattoos! 4-1-14

I woke up in this dream (in the dream) to discover I was covered with very bizarre tattoos; even 3 dimensional ones! I had been sleeping in a large room with many others and went around asking them what happened; how did I get the tattoos, but they didn't know.

On one leg was a 3-D ship and many small images and on the other leg was something like planets and stars. There were many other images all over my body I don't remember.

Breathing Underwater 10-26-10

This dream found me and a young woman (who I didn't recognize) diving underwater to fix something in a flooded house. Whatever it was took longer than we had figured when I noticed that we were somehow breathing! Afterwards I told some others we had learned to breathe underwater and the young woman and I went back down again.

Morphing People at the Farm 7-4-14

A few of us were doing something important in one of the old buildings at the farm house (moving things in and out?) one night, but were being sabotaged some way by some people hiding on the roof. I discovered them and grabbed a piece of electrical conduit and went after them. I hit one and the rest scattered. I went after the leader and spotted him hiding around a corner about 30 yards away.

I then chased him to the middle of the southeast cowyard before I caught him and his cohorts. I hit one big one and then concentrated on the leader, which to my shock, turned into a bull! I began to work him over with the conduit while his cohorts (who were also animals) cowered a short ways away!

Jesus to Fight the Adversary 8-17-14

I was looking down a long, dark, narrow, staircase leading to the street, when I heard someone down there say; *"Jesus is coming to fight the adversary"*. The weird thing is; they were talking about me! I then went down the staircase to the street. I felt the adversary's presence, but never engaged it.

The Prodigy 4-6-14

This dream opened with a group of us (including Judy) in what looked like a waiting room with couches all around. The strange thing was; I suddenly realized I was holding a tiny baby boy, about 3-5 lbs! I don't know who the mother was, but I knew it was mine. I'm not sure what we were waiting for, but we were tired and laid on the couches to sleep.

When we awoke, I was shocked to see the little boy was now about 2 ft tall and talking! I excitedly told everyone, but no one seemed interested. We then rearranged ourselves on the couches and went back to sleep. When we awoke again, the little boy was now about 10 and I knew there was something very special about him.

The next scene opened high in the night sky to see an explosion in the middle of a city. The shocking things was that out of the billowing smoke and debris cloud rode my son on something like a motorcycle followed by a troop of others!

www.ingramcontent.com/pod-product-compliance
Lightning Source LLC
Chambersburg PA
CBHW040824120726
48005CB00012B/1499